Edexcel

Leisure and Tourism

GCSE

Edexcel

Leisure and Tourism

GCSE

Diane Canwell

Jonathan Sutherland

Edexcel
Success through qualifications

Published in 2003 by:
Nelson Thornes Ltd
Delta Place
27 Bath Road
CHELTENHAM
GL53 7TH
United Kingdom

03 04 05 06 07 / 10 9 8 7 6 5 4 3 2 1

A catalogue record for this book is available from the British Library.

ISBN 0 7487 8031 9

Illustrations by Ian West, Derek Griffin and GreenGate Publishing Services
Page make-up by GreenGate Publishing Services, Tonbridge

Printed and bound in Spain by Graficas Estella

Acknowledgements

The authors and publisher would like to thank the following for permission to reproduce material:

The Institute of Sports Sponsorship for the extract on page 169; The Radio Advertising Bureau for the table on page 181.

Every effort has been made to contact copyright holders and we apologise if any have been overlooked.

Photo credits
- Action Plus Images p. 25, p. 26, p. 40, p. 45 bottom, p. 51, p. 113, p. 168 bottom, p. 169, p. 201
- Andes Press Agency p. 14, p. 39, p. 70
- Blockbuster p. 13
- Britain on View Picture Library p. 61, pp. 100–101
- Cheltenham Festivals & Entertainment p. 229
- Cheltenham Tourist Board p. 17 right, p. 180
- Chessington World Of Adventures 2003 p. 9 bottom
- Collections/Barry Payling p. 86 right
- Collections/Gary Smith p. 86 middle
- Collections/Geoff Howard p. 96 bottom
- Collections/Graham Burns p. 132
- Collections/Philip Craven p. 86 left
- Corbis/Ed Bock pp. 184–185
- Corbis/LWA Sharie Kennedy p. 204 left
- Corbis/Rob Lewine p. 208 right
- Corbis/Rolf Bruderer p. 222
- Corel 73 (NT) p. 8
- Corel 76 (NT) p. 68
- Corel 157 (NT) p. 75
- Corel 176 (NT) p. 216
- Corel 184 (NT) p. 74 bottom
- Corel 296 (NT) p. 56
- Corel 423 (NT) p. 40 bottom
- Corel 427 (NT) p. 38
- Corel 449 (NT) p. 30 top right
- Corel 604 (NT) p. 76
- Corel 627 (NT) p. 79
- Corel 630 (NT) p. 66
- Corel 636 (NT) p. 33 top right
- Corel 640 (NT) pp. 2–3

- Corel 641 (NT) p. 115, p. 158 top
- Corel 687 (NT) p. 173
- Corel 706 (NT) p. 17 left
- Corel 737 (NT) p. 191
- Corel 745 (NT) p. 7
- Corel 765 (NT) p. 158 bottom
- Corel 776 (NT) p. 42
- Corel 778 (NT) p. 37 left
- Corel 780 (NT) p. 55
- Corel 781 (NT) p. 126 right
- Corel 793 (NT) p. 126 left
- Digital Stock 1 (NT) p. 82
- Digital Vision 8 (NT) p. 72
- Digital Vision 11 (NT) p. 45 top
- DMG World Media p. 168 top
- DWP Comms Press Office p. 218 top
- Europcar Ltd p. 69
- Eurotunnel p. 78 bottom
- Image 100 37 (NT) p. 135
- Imagin Lon (NT) p. 15
- Ingram/IL V2 (NT) p. 36
- Intercontinental Hotel Group p. 57, p. 208 left
- Joe Cornish/Digital vision LL (NT) p. 93, p. 126 middle
- John Birdsall Photography p. 200 bottom, p. 223, p. 249 left
- John Walmsley Photography p. 47, p. 167, p. 203
- Lastminute.com p. 62
- Lever Faberge p. 165 right
- Madame Tussauds p. 105 top
- Marks & Spencer p. 147
- McDonald's Reastaurants Ltd p. 15 bottom
- National Express p. 81
- Peter Adams/Digital Vision BP (NT) p. 30 top left, p. 33 top left
- Photodisc 22 (NT) p. 94
- Photodisc 24 (NT) p. 33 bottom left
- Photodisc 40 (NT) p. 108 left, p. 207
- Photodisc 45 (NT) p. 9 top, p. 41
- Photodisc 66 (NT) p. 210
- Photodisc 67 (NT) p. 48, p. 110, p. 194
- Photodisc 68 (NT) p. 221
- Photodisc 71 (NT) p. 33 bottom middle, p. 225
- Photofusion/Bob Watkins p. 43
- Photofusion/Brenda Price p. 200 top, p. 226
- Photofusion/Caroline Mardo p. 202 top
- Photofusion/Christa Stadtler p. 108 right

- Photofusion/David Montford p. 131
- Photofusion/David Tothill p. 190
- Photofusion/Gary Parker p. 11
- Photofusion/Jacky Chapman p. 187
- Photofusion/Maggie Murray p. 152
- Photofusion/Paul Doyle p. 37, p. 193
- Photofusion/Paula Glassman p. 122 right
- Photofusion/Peter Olive p. 249 left
- Photofusion/Simin Ahmadi p. 34
- Photofusion/Ute Klaphake p. 153
- Pizza Express p. 231 bottom
- Pizza Hut/Freud Communications p. 15 middle, p. 145
- QBO Bell Pottinger p. 27
- Rex Features/Action Press p. 165 left
- Rex Features/Eva Mag p. 97
- Rex Features/Jonathan Player p. 122 left
- Rex Features/Kevin Wisniewski p. 204 right
- Rex Features/R Sowersby p. 206
- Rex Features/Times p. 53, p. 242
- Rubberball WW (NT) p. 33 bottom right, p. 49, p. 196, p. 243, p. 244
- Science & Society Picture Library p. 264
- Southampton Football Club p. 22
- Stockpix 3 (NT) p. 74 top
- The Eden Project p. 214
- The Highlands of Scotland Tourist Board p. 102 right
- The Southern & South East England Tourist Board p. 102 left
- Thomson Holidays p. 105 bottom, p. 107, p. 218, p. 228, p. 243
- Virgin p. 231 top
- Virgin Airways p. 95, p. 96 top
- Youth Hostel Association p. 65.

Introduction

This book has been written to assist students and teachers studying and delivering the GCSE leisure and tourism double award. As far as possible, every attempt has been made to concentrate on the practical side of learning about leisure and tourism. The businesses featured in the book are well known and have been chosen to demonstrate exactly how the leisure and tourism industry operates.

The book itself exactly matches the three units of the GCSE in leisure and tourism. The first unit is externally assessed through a formal examination. This unit has particularly emphasised key leisure and tourism jargon terms, aims and objectives. The assessment of the other two units involves students carrying out research and completing a report on the relevant aspect of the leisure and tourism industry. In these units the book aims to help build up the students' knowledge in order to help make their research task less complicated and to help them think about aspects that will need to be included in their portfolio of work.

Throughout the book 'jargon dragons' are used to explain unfamiliar words or terms associated with the leisure and tourism industry. The 'find it out' features suggest to the students how they could obtain more information and develop their research skills. 'Think it through' sections enable students to apply their knowledge to problems. There are also a number of case studies that are mostly examples from real-life leisure and tourism. These are accompanied by short questions and additional research tasks to help reinforce learning and understanding.

The Edexcel teacher pack is available to support this text which provides teachers with additional information, student worksheets and, where appropriate, suggested answers to questions posed within the book.

Jon Sutherland and Diane Canwell
March 2003

Investigating

What's in this unit?

This unit is about the importance of leisure and tourism in today's society. You will learn about the different organisations and facilities available to people, how the leisure and tourism industry works and how it offers a high level of service to customers. You will be able to investigate the facilities in a particular area and collect information to identify them as particular parts of the leisure and tourism industry.

You will also learn about the travel and tourism industry, studying the ways in which people travel and how the industry provides products and services for customers. You will develop an understanding about which of the tourist destinations in the United Kingdom are the most popular and be able to locate them on a map, state what they offer and identify how to reach them.

You will learn the difference between leisure and tourism and the links between the two industries. You will also know some geography and the types of jobs that are available in the industries.

This unit will prepare you for your assessment, which is a one-and-a-half hour externally set examination. In the examination you will be given case-study material to read and then have to answer questions from both leisure and travel and tourism.

Leisure and Tourism

1

In this unit you will learn about:

The leisure industry

THE JARGON DRAGON

leisure – the time that people have left after they have done all the things that they have to do, for instance when they have finished work or school

recreation – activities that people enjoy doing during their leisure time

<u>**Leisure**</u> is the time you spend not working or not going to school. It is not the same as free time as there are many jobs and other activities, such as sleeping, to do during these hours. Perhaps a better way of describing leisure is to refer to it as <u>**recreation**</u>. Recreation time is made up of the activities that people do during their leisure time.

There is a huge range of different ways to spend your recreation time.

Before we look at the different types of leisure and recreation activities, it is probably a good idea to put them into categories. The main types are:

- active, such as playing sports or walking;
- passive, such as reading or watching the television;
- home-based, such as listening to music or playing computer games;
- away from the home, such as going to the cinema or visiting a theme park.

You can use some of these categories together to describe different types of leisure and recreation. If you played football for a local team, it would be *active* and *away from home*, but if you just went to watch the local team play, it would be *passive* and *away from home*. It might be useful to think about these categories later when we look at the different types of activities and the places where people do them.

Think IT THROUGH

How do you spend your recreation time? Write a list of the things you do when all your jobs are finished. How much time do you have each week to spend on these recreations?

Let's use our four categories to see where some of the most popular leisure activities fit.

Leisure activity	Active	Passive	Home based	Away from the home
Reading				
Playing sport				
Watching sport				
Going to the cinema				
Going to a disco				
Walking				
Watching TV or listening to the radio				
Eating out				
Playing computer games				
Visiting a tourist attraction				

Recent research has shown that the health-and-fitness industry alone is worth £931 million a year. Its popularity has nearly doubled in the last five years. The favourite **active** recreational activity is fitness and running and one in five of the population takes up a new sport each year. This means that the fastest growing area of leisure involves sports goods and toys and is worth around £6.25 billion per year. Leisure is not just about being active. Watching television is by far the most popular **passive** recreational activity.

FIND IT OUT

Your local council should have its own website where you will find a list of the local recreation or leisure facilities, such as swimming pools, leisure centres and museums. They may even have some information about how much each of these facilities is used. Try to find out which is the most popular local recreational facility. Do you use it yourself? Do other students use it? Ask them if they do.

You will be able to find your local council's website at this address:

www.tagish.co.uk/tagish/links/localgov.htm

The key components of the leisure industry

It is useful to categorise the many different activities and facilities within the leisure industry. These categories are known as the key components of the industry.

THE JARGON DRAGON

participate – take an active part in

Sport and physical recreation

It has been estimated that around 29 million people regularly **participate** in sport or physical recreation in the United Kingdom. This includes everything from rugby to country dancing and from cross-country walking to motor racing. There are an estimated 150 000 sports clubs in the United Kingdom alone.

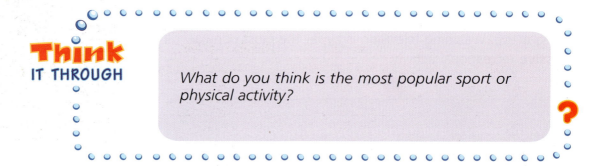

Think IT THROUGH

What do you think is the most popular sport or physical activity?

You would be wrong to believe that football is the most popular participation sport. In fact it is only seventh in the top 10 participation sports.

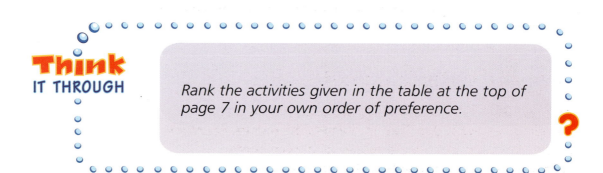

Think IT THROUGH

Rank the activities given in the table at the top of page 7 in your own order of preference.

Adults participating at least once a month, 1996 (%)			School children participating at least once a year, 1994 (%)		
1.	Walking	44.5	1.	Swimming	85
2.	Swimming	14.6	2.	Athletics (track and field)	81
3.	Keep fit/yoga	12.3	3.	Cycling	79
4.	Snooker/billiards	11.3	4.	Football	77
5.	Cycling	11	5.	Rounders	75
6.	Weight training	5.6	6.	Gymnastics (gym)	69
7.	Football	4.8	7.	Tennis	67
8.	Golf	4.7	8.	Walking (>1hr)/hiking	62
9.	Running	4.5	9.	Cricket	59
10.	Tenpin bowls/skittles	3.4	10.	Cross country/jogging	51

Source: Office of Population Censuses and Surveys, *Living in Britain*, 1996.

Source: Sports Council, *Young People and Sport in England*, 1994.

There is another way to measure the popularity of the sport and that is by looking at the number of people who are members of clubs and how many clubs there are for each of the sports. The latest figures are for 1995.

		Members	Number of clubs
1.	Football	1 650 000	42 000
2.	Billiards/snooker	1 500 000	5 300
3.	Golf	1 217 000	2 877
4.	Tennis	750 000	2 450
5.	Bowls	500 000	8 600
6.	Sailing	450 000	1 620
7.	Motor sports	420 000	750
8.	Rugby union	284 000	2 026
9.	Martial arts	175 000	1 000
10.	Hockey	90 000	2 000
11.	Athletics	135 000	1 750

Source: based on information from www.sportengland.org

Arts and entertainment

Around 135 million people go to the cinema each year, spending nearly £500 million. In theatres the musical *Phantom of the Opera* has taken more money at the box office worldwide than any film ever, including *Titanic*.

Countryside recreation

There are dozens of outdoor pursuits in addition to walking or cycling. These include fishing, hunting and shooting, camping, caving, mountaineering, most motor sports and orienteering. Countryside recreation is very important as it is worth £12 billion per year and provides 380 000 jobs. In the United Kingdom visitors make 15 million trips to the countryside each year.

Home-based leisure

Home-based leisure activities include things that we do both inside and outside the house. Gardening and do-it-yourself, which are both very popular, are also counted as home-based leisure activities.

Participation in home-based leisure activities in the United Kingdom by gender and age

	16–19	20–24	25–34	35–44	45–54	55–64	65 and over	Percentages (aged 16 and over)
Males								
Watching TV	99	99	99	99	99	100	98	99
Visiting/entertaining friends or relations	97	97	97	96	94	94	92	95
Listening to radio	93	92	94	93	92	86	79	89
Listening to CDs/tapes	97	96	92	86	78	69	54	78
Reading books	51	59	58	61	57	59	58	58
Gardening	20	21	42	55	58	63	62	52
DIY	33	40	66	67	63	61	46	57
Dressmaking/needlework/knitting	4	4	4	3	3	3	3	3
Females								
Watching TV	99	98	99	98	99	99	99	99
Visiting/entertaining friends or relations	98	99	99	97	97	96	94	97
Listening to radio	97	95	92	89	86	83	77	87
Listening to CDs/tapes	99	96	92	89	79	65	47	77
Reading books	74	71	69	72	73	71	68	71
Gardening	10	21	40	52	58	56	43	45
DIY	16	28	40	38	36	25	13	29
Dressmaking/needlework/knitting	15	23	29	37	44	48	39	36

Sources: General Household Survey, Office for National Statistics; Continuous Household Survey, Northern Ireland Statistics and Research Agency

Children's play activities

Most local areas have playgrounds, adventure playgrounds and play schemes for children. It is difficult to calculate the number of schemes and playgrounds in the United Kingdom, although they are popular and much used. Some, particularly the play schemes, which are usually run during school holidays, are supervised by adults.

Visitor attractions

There are 500 000 **listed buildings** of historical importance in the United Kingdom, nearly 18 000 monuments and 8500 **conservation areas**. These are all popular visitor attractions. In other words, they are popular for people to visit on a day out.

Theme parks attract around 12.5 million people each year. The most popular is Alton Towers, followed by Chessington World of Adventure and Legoland. One ride can cost as much as £5 million to build. However, more people choose to go to museums than theme parks or music concerts.

THE JARGON DRAGON

listed building – this refers to a house or other building that, because of its great historical importance, cannot be changed by the owner

conservation area – this refers to a particular part of a town, city or piece of countryside that the country considers too beautiful or too important to change

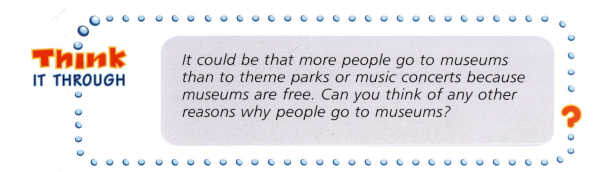

Think IT THROUGH

It could be that more people go to museums than to theme parks or music concerts because museums are free. Can you think of any other reasons why people go to museums?

THE JARGON DRAGON

catering – providing food and drink for sale to the general public

Catering

Catering, as a whole, is worth £47.8 billion per year, of which £16.2 billion comes from clubs, pubs and wine bars.

In 2000 there were 11 195 hotels in the United Kingdom, 51 472 restaurants, 45 230 pubs and 4701 other types of catering establishments. In total, all the different types of catering establishments employed 1 765 000 people.

Facilities in the leisure industry

In addition to the more famous national leisure facilities in the country, you should not forget that there are many local leisure industries that provide facilities for the local population.

Local leisure centres and health clubs

Local councils often have a leisure centre that usually offers indoor and, perhaps, some outdoor facilities. Typically you will find five-a-side football, basketball, badminton courts and possibly a swimming pool within a leisure centre. These centres are also useful places for classes and clubs, which may include keep-fit classes, martial arts classes (such as judo) and indoor bowling classes.

The most common leisure activities in the United Kingdom are home based or social, including entertaining or visiting relatives and friends. As 97% of all households have colour televisions, watching television is by far the most popular leisure activity. Around 60% of the country's population are members of public libraries and reading books is still a very popular pastime, as is listening to the radio and to music. Over 60% of all homes have a CD player.

In 1999 alone, United Kingdom residents took 134 million trips within their own country. The most popular destinations were to the West Country, eastern England, Scotland and Wales. In the same year, United Kingdom residents made over 53 million visits to other countries. The most popular short-haul destination was Spain, followed by France. The most popular long-haul holidays were to Central and South America and the Caribbean.

(Based on www.britain.org.nz)

Q1 *Most of your class will have a colour television. Find out how many hours a week people in your classmates' homes watch television. Copy this information into a computer spreadsheet so you can find the average time people watch television per week.*

Q2 *Ask the members of your class which places in the United Kingdom they have visited in the past year. Find out which was the most popular destination.*

Q3 *Find out what 'long haul' and 'short haul' mean. Give some examples of long- and short-haul destinations from the United Kingdom.*

Find out what is on offer at your local leisure centre. What kind of classes do they run? In which different activities can you participate?

THE JARGON DRAGON

Privately run – not owned by a local council but owned by an individual or group of individuals

Over the last few years a large number of **privately run** health clubs were set up across the country. Like some of the council-run leisure centres, you will need to be a member in order to use the facilities of the health club. These health clubs are private businesses and usually charge a large subscription to their members so they can often afford the most up-to-date equipment, such as heart-monitoring machines.

Look in the Yellow Pages and see how many health clubs you can find in your local area. Are they privately run or does the local council own them? See if you can find out what they charge for membership. How much would a member have to pay to hire their equipment for an hour?

Local libraries

Libraries are another facility provided by local councils. You have to be a member in order to borrow books. There are some books that you will only be able to use in the library itself. These are known as reference books.

Libraries often have most national and all local newspapers and, if the library does not have the book you are looking for, then it can order it from another library. Many libraries now have computer facilities and Internet access, as well as videos, CDs and music tapes.

Libraries advertise local attractions and forthcoming events in the immediate area. This is useful for visitors to the area.

Visit your local library and ask for a leaflet that details all of the services and facilities that it offers. Also, find out:

1. *what you have to do to become a member of your local library;*
2. *how much you have to pay if you return a book late.*

Local video and DVD-rental shops

Most areas have video rental shops that work rather like libraries. The major difference is that you pay for every item you borrow. Most of these shops offer videos, DVDs and computer games (usually for PlayStation, X-box, Game Cube and perhaps others). Normally you will not only need to be a member but you will also be expected to pay for every day that you borrow or hire the video, DVD or computer game.

Bringing Entertainment Home
www.blockbuster.co.uk

It is now also possible to borrow DVDs via the Internet. The DVDs are posted to you and you borrow them for one week and then mail them back. One example of this service can be found at www.movietrak.com

Because watching videos at home has become a popular way of spending leisure time, larger video shops make extra money by selling drinks, popcorn, chocolate and ice-cream.

Can you think of places in your local area where you can hire videos? Do they sell drinks and sweets? Do you have to be a member to hire a video?

Think
IT THROUGH

Local cinemas and theatres

As television became more popular and cheaper, many cinemas and theatres closed – but now cinemas and theatres are enjoying their greatest popularity for 50 years. Many new cinemas have been opened and the number of people attending theatres has increased.

Cinemas try to offer as wide a range of new movies as possible. This is why each cinema within the complex is actually quite small and some of the bigger cinemas may have as many as 20 or more screens. In this way customers can see the movies they want to see and can have more choice about when they go to see them. Cinemas offer customers the chance to buy their tickets either online or via the telephone and many of them not only sell drinks and food but also have bars, restaurants and shops within the complex. These shops often sell movie-related items and souvenirs and cinema membership cards.

FIND IT OUT

Is there a cinema complex in your local area? If so, find out how many movies are being shown this week. What else does the cinema sell its customers? You might find these websites useful: www.odeon.co.uk and www.warnerbrothers.com.

Theatres may offer local **amateur** productions of plays, musicals and dramas, or touring productions can visit and put on their show for a number of days or sometimes weeks. Many theatres are also places where live music concerts are featured. Bands that tour the country will be able to find theatres in most areas where they can put on a performance for fans living in that area.

THE JARGON DRAGON

amateur – this means the opposite of professional and those involved do not get paid

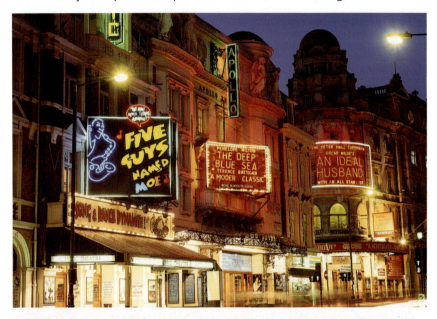

What productions will your local theatre offer this season? You could find this information either at your local library or by searching for the name of the theatre on the Internet. The theatre will present its timetable of productions for several months in advance. Do you think going to the theatre is more expensive than going to the cinema, or less?

Find out the different prices and compare.

FIND IT OUT

Local pubs, restaurants and takeaway restaurants

In addition to selling drink and food, many public houses also offer entertainment to their customers. These are either events that they can watch or listen to, such as musicians, or events in which they can participate, such as quiz nights. Some also have games machines, dartboards or pool tables.

ethnic - relating to different races of people from different places

Takeaway restaurants often offer home delivery services and in most local areas customers will be able to find a wide range of different **ethnic** takeaways (for example, offering Chinese, Indian, Turkish, Greek or Italian food).

FIND IT OUT

How many different takeaway restaurants do you have in your local area? Write a list of those you know about and look in the Yellow Pages to see if you can add to your list.

See if you can find out if they provide a home delivery service. Do they have any special offers on at the moment? Sometimes they offer cheaper meals on weekday evenings.

Local community centres

There are thousands of community centres around the country, usually owned and run by the local councils. These community centres are available to rent so that classes, playgroups, workgroups or clubs can be held on a regular basis. Many of the community centres have kitchens and staff to provide refreshments.

Think IT THROUGH

How many community centres are there in your local area? Where are they located? Often you will find them located in areas of high population, or sometimes near to schools or colleges. Why do you think they are located where they are? What are they used for?

Local museums and galleries

There are hundreds of local museums that feature items from the area's past. Some of these local museums may have special collections and they may be known nationally as being the major museum and experts in a particular area. These special collections may include photographs from the past or examples of items used during a particular period. A good example of a local museum is the Bethnal Green Toy Museum.

Local art galleries offer artists and sculptors the opportunity to display their work to the public, either in the hope that they will be able to sell them, or to give others the opportunity to view their work.

Does your local area have an art gallery? If so, what type of art does it exhibit? Do only local artists exhibit their work there?

Think
IT THROUGH

Local sports venues

Local councils provide most local sports venues and these may be a part of a leisure centre. Other sports venues may be parts of parks that have been put aside for a particular sport.

The council will look after these sports venues so that the local people can use them. A typical example of this is football pitches, which can be used by local amateur teams to play games on Saturdays or Sundays.

Some areas have athletics facilities, including running tracks, sandpits for long jump and high jump as well as the necessary equipment, for example hurdles. Some areas are also fortunate enough to have all-weather or night-time facilities. Astro Turf, an artificial soft surface that looks like grass, can be laid so that football, tennis or basketball can be played whatever the weather. In many cases these areas also have floodlighting so that games can be played after dark.

Full-size swimming pools can also be counted as sports venues. Amateur swimming events and practice sessions are often held here.

FIND IT OUT

Where is the nearest local place that someone could go to ice-skate or play ice hockey? Where is the nearest place where someone could go to practise scuba or sub-aqua diving? How much would it cost to do these activities?

National leisure facilities

Many national leisure facilities are so important that people are prepared to travel long distances to use them. The national leisure facilities are recognised as being the leaders in their field in supporting particular kinds of sports. However, many of the larger cities such as Leeds, Nottingham and London have facilities that now rival them in terms of what they have on offer.

Recreation centres

Recreation centres are training grounds or centres of excellence used by the country's leading sportsmen and sportswomen. These are the most famous:

Bisham Abbey – near Marlow, Buckinghamshire
www.nationalsportscentres.co.uk/bisham_abbey/index.htm

Purpose – facilities for tennis, hockey, football, rugby, weightlifting, judo, rowing and sailing.

Facilities:

- seven outdoor floodlit tennis courts;
- four indoor tennis courts – 89 m × 45 m;
- three clay tennis courts;
- one grass tennis court;
- floodlit artificial turf pitch - 131 m × 116 m;
- two football pitches;
- one rugby pitch;
- weightlifting competition hall – 19 m × 14 m;
- two squash courts;
- sailing school;
- Harper's fitness club;
- group training studio;
- nine-hole golf course;
- seven conference and banqueting rooms;
- 44 bedrooms (94 beds);
- bar, catering and function facilities.

Crystal Palace – London
www.nationalsportscentres.co.uk/crystal/index.htm

Purpose – facilities for nearly every type of indoor or outdoor sport.

Facilities:

- athletics stadium – floodlit 400 m eight-lane track with warm-up areas and central grass area for football, rugby and American football, plus seating for 16 500;
- two synthetic artificial turf pitches – 87.5 m × 49.5 m and 109 × 60 m;
- covered practice area – 34.14 m × 21.33 m;
- one grass pitch;

- four tennis courts (also used for netball);
- four swimming pools – racing (50 m, eight lane with seating for 1800) diving (1 m and 3 m springboards plus 5 m, 7.5 m and 10 m platforms), teaching (18.26 m long) and training (25 m, six lane);
- indoor track – 100 m × 10 m with jump and pole-vaulting areas;
- multi-purpose indoor arena with seating for 2100;
- four badminton courts;
- five squash courts;
- two training halls;
- boxing hall;
- two dedicated weight training rooms;
- Harper's fitness club;
- group training studio;
- climbing wall;
- three conference /meeting rooms;
- 86 bedrooms (135 beds);
- bar, catering and function facilities.

Glenmore Lodge – Aviemore, Invernessshire

www.glenmorelodge.org.uk

Purpose – mountain biking, running, walking and orienteering.

Facilities:

- indoor climbing wall;
- canoe rolling pool;
- gym;
- sports and remedial massage;
- physiotherapy.

Holme Pierre Pont (National Water-sports Centre) – Holme Pierre Pont, Nottingham

www.nationalsportscentres.co.uk/hpp/index.htm

Purpose – all water sports, including rowing, canoeing and waterskiing.

Facilities:

- regatta lake – 2000 m × 135 m;
- canoe slalom course;
- water ski lagoon – includes cable tow;

- multi-purpose sports hall – 26 m x 16 m;
- fitness training centre;
- six conference and banqueting rooms;
- 35 bedrooms (78 beds);
- bar, catering and function facilities.

Lilleshall – near Newport, Shropshire

www.nationalsportscentres.co.uk/lilleshall/index.htm

Purpose – hockey, cricket, squash, movement and dance and other sports.

Facilities:

- four outdoor floodlit tennis courts;
- three grass tennis courts;
- gymnastics training hall – 35 m x 36 m;
- specialist pitted gymnastics training hall – 27 m x 35 m;
- multi-purpose sports hall – 37.5 m x 32 m;
- general-purpose sports hall – 21 m x 24 m;
- specialist gymnasium;
- five squash courts;
- weight training room;
- bowls lawn;
- 35 acres of grass pitches;
- studio hall (weekends only) – 21 m x 24 m;
- floodlit artificial turf pitch – 140 m x 77 m;
- cricket/archery – 92 m x 11.5 m;
- fifteen conference and banqueting rooms;
- bar, catering and function rooms;
- 80 bedrooms (187 beds).

Plas-y-Brenin (National Mountain Centre) – Capel Curig, Gwynedd

www.pyb.co.uk

Purpose – hill walking, climbing, mountaineering, ski touring, kayaking and canoeing.

Facilities:

- climbing wall;
- training wall;
- ski slope;
- canoe pool;
- equipment hire;
- self-catering accommodation;
- bar.

Go to the website of each of the recreation centres we have given you. Find out, for each:

- When was it first set up?
- What other organisations is it linked to?

National sports venues

The United Kingdom's most popular sports need large stadiums for the enormous numbers of people who are interested in watching them live.

Southampton Football Club

Soccer stadiums

Soccer is another word for football, or association football. At this moment England does not have a national stadium as it is being rebuilt at Wembley in London. The Millennium Stadium, which is featured under 'rugby stadiums' below, is being used as the national stadium for events such as the FA Cup Final and the Nationwide Playoff Finals. At present England's international football fixtures are being played at the main premiership stadiums around the country.

Hampden Park, Glasgow, Scotland. Ground capacity: 52 000. Hampden Park is the home of the Scottish national football team; it has the world's first national football museum. It was rebuilt in 1999 and is currently having the east stand redeveloped. The ground does not only host football – concerts and American football matches have also been known to take place there. Stadium officials estimated that one million people visited the stadium during 2001.

At the time of writing the following teams are in the English premiership. Each season three teams are relegated to the Nationwide Division One and three other teams replace them.

Club name	Ground name	Ground capacity	Record gate	Location
Arsenal	Highbury	38 900 /visitors' allocation 2900	73 295 v Sunderland (Div 1) 9 Mar 1935	London
Aston Villa	Villa Park	43 000 /visitors' allocation 2983	76 588 v Derby (FA Cup) 2 Mar 1946	West Midlands
Birmingham City	St Andrews	30 016/visitors' allocation up to 4500	67 341 v Everton (FA Cup) 11 Feb 1939	West Midlands
Blackburn Rovers	Ewood Park	31 367/visitors' allocation 3914	61 783 v Bolton (FA Cup) 2 Mar 1929	Blackburn
Bolton Wanderers	Reebok Stadium	27 800/visitors' allocation 5200	69 912 v Manchester City (FA Cup) 18 Feb 1933	Greater Manchester
Charlton Athletic	The Valley	26 500/visitors' allocation up to 2000	75 031 v Aston Villa (FA Cup) 12 Feb 1938	London
Chelsea	Stamford Bridge	42 500/visitors' allocation up to 3200	82 905 v Arsenal (Div 1) 12 Oct 1935	London
Everton	Goodison Park	40 260/visitors' allocation 2726	78 299 v Liverpool (Div 1) 18 Sept 1948	Liverpool
Fulham	Craven Cottage (currently playing at Queen's Park Rangers' Loftus Road)	18 623 (7023 seats)/ visitors' allocation 4600	49 335 v Millwall (Div 2) 8 October 1938	London
Leeds United	Elland Road	40 245/visitors' allocation 3600	57 892 v Sunderland (FA Cup Rd 5 replay) 15 March 1967	Leeds
Leicester City	Walkers Stadium	32 500/visitors' allocation 3000	47 298 v Tottenham Hotspur 18 Feb 1928	Leicester
Liverpool	Anfield	45 362/visitors' allocation 1972	61 905 v Wolves (FA Cup) 2 Feb 1952	Liverpool
Manchester City	Maine Road	34 000/visitors' allocation up to 3200	84 569 v Stoke (FA Cup Quarter-Final) 3 Mar 1934	Manchester
Manchester United	Old Trafford	67 700/visitors' allocation up to 3000	76 962 Wolves v Grimsby (FA Cup Semi-Final) 25 Mar 1939	Manchester
Middlesbrough	Riverside	35 100/visitors' allocation 3450	30 228 v Oxford United (Div 1) 3 May 1998	Middlesbrough
Newcastle United	St James Park	52 000/visitors' allocation up to 3000	68 386 v Chelsea (Div 1) 3 Sept 1930	Newcastle
Portsmouth	Fratton Park	19 214/visitors' allocation 3121	51 385 v Derby County 1949	Portsmouth
Southampton	Saint Mary's	32 251/visitors' allocation 3000	31 973 v Newcastle (Premier League) 11 May 2002	Southampton
Tottenham Hotspur	White Hart Lane	36 257/visitors' allocation 3000	73 038 v Sunderland (FA Cup) 5 Mar 1938	London
Wolverhampton Wanderers	Molineux Stadium	28 525/visitors' allocation 4528	63 315 v Liverpool (FA Cup) 11 Feb 1939	West Midlands

Windsor Park, 20 Windsor Avenue, Belfast. Ground capacity: 20 332. This is different from all of the other stadiums that play host to our national teams in the British Isles, the reason being that it is owned by Linfield FC and the Northern Irish national side borrows it for its international home matches.

Find the official team website for at least three of the principal premiership stadiums given in the table above. For each one you will also need to find:

- how to get there by train or coach;
- the cost for two adults and two children to attend a match;
- the cost of a programme;
- the cost of a team home shirt.

Rugby stadiums

Millennium Stadium, 101 St Mary's Street, Cardiff. Ground capacity: 72 000. At a cost of £130 million the Millennium Stadium was completed in October 1999. While Wembley is being redeveloped (until 2005) this stadium has been awarded the English domestic cup finals as well as a host of other events.

Murrayfield, Edinburgh. Capacity: 67 500. Murrayfield is one of the largest and most impressive stadiums in the United Kingdom. It was first opened in 1925 and was to be the home of Scottish Rugby Union. Over the years Murrayfield has seen some gigantic crowds including a world record rugby crowd of over 104 000 in 1975 to see the Scottish rugby team play Wales in the Five Nations tournament.

Twickenham, Rugby Road, Twickenham, Middlesex. Capacity: 75 000. The Rugby Football Union (RFU) has unveiled plans to build a new South Stand at Twickenham Stadium. These plans will increase the capacity of the West London stadium from 75 000 to 82 000. The ambitious plans will see all four sides of the stadium finally joined up and also include a 200-bed hotel, conference and exhibition space, a health-and-fitness club, increased office space for the RFU and a new shop.

FIND IT OUT

Find Twickenham on a map of the United Kingdom.

1. *What would be the best method of transport for you from your home?*
2. *Write a list of the different methods of transport you may have to use to get there.*
3. *How long do you think it would take you to get there?*

Cricket stadiums

Lord's Cricket Ground, St John's Wood, London. Lord's is the 'home of cricket' and its owner, Marylebone Cricket Club (MCC), remains the guardian of both the laws and the spirit of cricket, and MCC sides (which play almost 500 games a year) perform a key role in promoting cricket. Lord's is the home of Middlesex County Cricket Club, the England and Wales Cricket Board (ECB) and the International Cricket Council (ICC).

Find Lord's Cricket Ground on a map of the United Kingdom. Now decide:

1. *What would be the best method of transport for you from your home?*
2. *Write a list of the different methods of transport you may have to use to get there.*
3. *How long do you think it would take you to get there?*

Hockey stadiums

Central Milton Keynes Hockey Stadium, The National Hockey Stadium, Silbury Road, Central Milton Keynes. The National Hockey Stadium is the international home of the sport of hockey. In recent months, the stadium has been linked with Wimbledon football club, which may move there as it has no stadium of its own.

Tennis stadiums

Tim Henman

Wimbledon, The All England Lawn Tennis and Croquet Club, Church Road, Wimbledon, London. Home of the All England Lawn Tennis and Croquet Club, the lawn tennis championships at Wimbledon have developed from the first event in 1877, viewed by a few hundred spectators, to a professional tournament attracting over 450 000 people. Through the press, radio, the Internet and television, millions of people watch the event throughout the world. The tournament starts each year six weeks before the first Monday in August and lasts for a fortnight or for as long as necessary to complete all events. Players from over 60 nations regularly compete.

Find a map of the London Underground. If you were at Liverpool Street Station, which tube lines would you need to take to get to Wimbledon? How many stops are involved between Liverpool Street and Wimbledon?

Wimbledon

National museums and galleries

There are hundreds of museums and galleries around the country. The table on page 28 lists some of the most famous and the largest in the country.

Visit the websites of two of the museums or galleries and find out:

1. *How much does it cost you, as a student, to enter?*
2. *What is their current temporary exhibition?*
3. *How much travel would be involved for you in getting there?*

Major visitor attractions

Many of the major visitor attractions in the United Kingdom are located in towns or cities that are of historic interest or are visitor attractions in their own right. The major visit attractions tend to be located where there is a large population, or good travel links to that location. These major attractions range from zoos to piers and towers. The table on the following pages gives you the major visitor attractions in the United Kingdom.

Museum or gallery	Collection	Location	Website
Beamish	The North of England Open Air Museum. Set in over 300 acres of countryside, it recreates life in the north of England in the early 1800s and 1900s.	The North of England Open Air Museum, Beamish, County Durham, DH9 0RG	www.beamish.org.uk
British Museum	Houses a vast collection of world art and artefacts.	The British Museum, Great Russell Street, London, WC1B 3DG	www.thebritishmuseum.ac.uk
Ironbridge Gorge	Ironbridge covers six square miles of the Ironbridge Gorge near Telford. The Ironbridge Gorge Museum Trust has eight museums covering a total of 80 acres. The Iron Bridge and Tollhouse, Blists Hill Victorian Town, Museum of Iron and Darby Furnace, the Darby Houses, Museum of the Gorge, Coalport China Museum, Jackfield Tile Museum, Broseley Pipeworks, Clay Tobacco Pipe Museum and the Teddy Bear Shop.	Ironbridge Gorge Museums, Ironbridge, Telford, Shropshire, TF8 7AW	www.ironbridge.org.uk
National Gallery	Collection of around 2300 Western European paintings from 1250 to 1900.	The National Gallery, Trafalgar Square, London, WC2N 5DN	www.nationalgallery.org.uk
National Museum of Photography, Film & Television	Founded in 1983, the National Museum of Photography, Film and Television quickly became the most visited national museum outside London, attracting approximately 750 000 visitors each year. The museum's collection includes more than three million items of historical, social and cultural value.	National Museum of Photography, Film & Television, Bradford, West Yorkshire, BD1 1NQ	www.nmpft.org.uk
National Railway Museum	The collection, including 103 locomotives and 177 other items of rolling stock, tells the railway story from Rocket to Eurostar.	National Railway Museum, Leeman Road, York, YO26 4XJ	www.nrm.org.uk
Natural History Museum	Dating from around 1860, the museum contains the national collection of geology and natural sciences.	The Natural History Museum, Cromwell Road, London, SW7 5BD	www.nhm.ac.uk
Science Museum	Opened in 1857 to house collections of transport, agricultural machinery, photography, film and television.	The Science Museum, Exhibition Road, South Kensington, London, SW7 2DD	www.sciencemuseum.org.uk
Tate Gallery	A series of three galleries, Tate Britain is the national gallery of British art from 1500 to the present day. Tate Liverpool is the home of the National Collection of Modern Art in the North of England and the largest gallery of modern and contemporary art outside London. Tate St Ives opened in June 1993 and offers an introduction to modern art.	Tate Britain, Millbank, London, SW1P 4RG; Tate Liverpool, Albert Dock, Liverpool, L3 4BB; Tate St Ives, Porthmeor Beach, St Ives, Cornwall TR26 1TG	www.tate.org.uk
Tate Modern	Tate Modern is Britain's new national museum of modern art.	Tate Modern, Bankside, London, SE1 9TG	www.tate.org.uk/modern
The Royal Armouries	The displays contain many of the examples of royal arms and armour in the Royal Armouries collection, including armours of Henry VIII, Charles I, Charles II and James II. Now in three locations.	Royal Armouries, Tower of London, London, EC3N 4AB; Royal Armouries Museum, Armouries Drive, Leeds, LS10 1LT; Fort Nelson Down End Road, Fareham Hants, PO17 6AN	www.armouries.org.uk

Major visitor attractions	Main features	Location	Website
Blackpool Tower and Pleasure Beach	Blackpool Tower is 518 ft 9 ins tall, weighs 2586 tons, was completed in 1894 and the lift makes over 50 000 trips a year. The Pleasure Beach has five roller coasters including a twin track racer. Set in 42 acres a host of attractions are available from travelling to the times of the dinosaurs, Alice in Wonderland, the Greatest Show on Earth, the Log Flume and Funshineland.	Blackpool Tower, The Promenade, Blackpool, FY1 4BJ	www.tourist-information-uk.com/blackpool-tower-pleasure-beach.htm
Bristol Zoo	Houses over 300 species from lions to dung beetles.	Bristol Zoo Gardens, Clifton, Bristol BS8 3HA	www.bristolzoo.org.uk
Chester Zoo	Run by the North of England Zoological Society, it has recently celebrated its one millionth visitor.	Chester Zoo, Chester, Cheshire, CH2 1LH	www.demon.co.uk/chesterzoo
Jorvik Viking Centre	The Jorvik Viking Centre in York opened in April 1984 and has since had over 12 million visitors. Here, archaeologists discovered the preserved remains of Viking Jorvik.	Coppergate, York, North Yorkshire, YO1 9WT	www.jorvik-viking-centre.co.uk
London Eye	British Airways' London Eye is the world's highest observation wheel and offers passengers views of Britain's capital city. The Eye takes guests on a 30-minute flight, rising to 450 feet above the river Thames, in 32 'high tech' fully enclosed capsules.	Nearest tube Westminster. The Eye is a 10 min walk across Westminster Bridge and along the South Bank	www.londoneye.com
London Zoo	The world's first scientific zoo, which opened in 1828.	London Zoo, Regent's Park, London NW1 4RY	www.londonzoo.org
Longleat Safari Park	The park is divided into eight main sections: The East African Reserve, Elephant Country, Monkey Jungle, Big Game Park, Deer Park, Tiger Territory, Lion Country and Wolf Wood.	Warminster, Wiltshire, BA12 7NW	www.longleat.co.uk
Madame Tussaud's	Waxworks, also in New York, Amsterdam, Hong Kong and Las Vegas.	Marylebone Road, London	www.madame-tussauds.com
NEC, Birmingham	The National Exhibition Centre is the busiest exhibition centre in Europe, staging more than 180 exhibitions each year, ranging from world-famous public shows such as Crufts Dog Show and the British International Motor Show to international trade exhibitions like IPEX and Spring Fair, Birmingham.	The NEC, Birmingham, B40 1NT	www.necgroup.co.uk/nec
Palace Pier, Brighton	Now renamed Brighton Pier. Completed in 1901 at a cost of £137 000, Brighton's Palace Pier was designed by R. St. G. Moore and measures 1760 feet (537 metres) long and 189 feet (58 metres) at its widest point. It has a Palace of Fun, amusements, bar, restaurant and shops.	Madeira Drive, Brighton, East Sussex, BN2 1TW	www.brightonpier.co.uk
Woburn Safari Park	Rhino, antelope, giraffe, lion, wolves, black bear and many more creatures.	Woburn Park, Woburn, Milton Keynes, Buckinghamshire, MK17 9QN	www.woburnsafari.co.uk

The London Eye

Blackpool Tower

FIND IT OUT

Visit at least three of the websites of the major visitor attractions we have given you in the table above. For each one find out:

1. How much would it cost you, as a student, to enter?

2. How much would it cost for a family of two adults and two children to enter?

3. If you were to spend a weekend close to one of these sites, is there another attraction within easy travelling distance that you could visit on the second day?

Theme parks

Theme parks are quite new to the United Kingdom but now there are dozens dotted around the country. Theme parks are like enormous funfairs and once you have paid the entrance fee at the gate all of the rides and attractions are free. They are called theme parks because each of the parks is usually split up into different zones. All of the rides and attractions in these zones are decorated in the same way, for example with a jungle theme or a space theme. Many of the parks offer two-day passes or even season tickets and many now have their own hotels. One of the most important attributes of a theme park is that it is near a large population or that it has very good transport links to the rest of the country.

Theme parks	Main features	Location	Website
Alton Towers	Alton Towers is divided into several themed areas, from Merrie England, the African village called Katanga Canyon and X-Sector.	Alton Towers, Alton, Staffordshire, ST10 4DB	www.alton-towers.co.uk
Camelot	Set in over 140 acres of Lancashire countryside, the site attracts over a million visitors annually. Camelot Theme Park, named the North West visitor attraction of the year in 1999 and Lancashire family attraction of the year 2002.	Charnock Richard, Chorley, Lancashire	www.camelottheme park.co.uk
Chessington World of Adventures	Themed areas including Animal Adventures, Beanoland, Forbidden Kingdom, Mexicana, Mystic East, Pirates' Cove, Toytown and Transylvania.	The Tussauds Group, Freepost SEA 1471, Chessington, KT9 2BR	www.chessington.co.uk
Legoland	Aimed at children aged 2–12 with over 50 interactive rides, live shows, building workshops, driving schools and attractions and set in 150 acres.	Winkfield Road, Windsor, Berkshire, SL4 4AY	www.lego.com/eng/legoland/windsor/default.asp
Thorpe Park	In 1998 Thorpe Park was bought by The Tussauds Group, one of Europe's largest operators and developers of visitor attractions. Thorpe Park remains one of Europe's leading leisure parks, with constantly rising visitor numbers. The past decade, in particular, has seen a huge change from what was originally an exhibition-style park to a highly successful leisure attraction particularly popular amongst the family market.	The Tussauds Group, Freepost SEA 1471, Chessington, KT9 2BR	www.thorpepark.co.uk

Choose three of the theme parks given above. For each one find out:

1. the cost of a one-day pass for you, as a student;

2. the name of the latest ride at the theme park;

3. how many different themed zones there are.

FIND IT OUT

Historical sites

Historical buildings are dotted around the United Kingdom and include castles, cathedrals, abbeys, churches and other buildings of interest. English Heritage looks after many of these sites and preserves them for future generations. The National Trust alone looks after over 140 country houses which keep important collections of art and treasures.

Historic site	Main features	Location	Website
Beaulieu	National Motor Museum, Palace House and Beaulieu Abbey. Attractions include collection of classic, vintage, and veteran motor cars and bikes, palace and gardens, abbey.	Beaulieu, Brockenhurst, Hampshire, SO42 7ZN	www.beaulieu.co.uk
Buckingham Palace	Buckingham Palace has served as the official London residence of Britain's sovereigns since 1837. It evolved from a town house that was owned from the beginning of the eighteenth century by the Dukes of Buckingham. Today it is the Queen's official residence.	Ticket Sales and Information Office, The Official Residences of The Queen, London, SW1A 1AA	www.royal.gov.uk
Chatsworth House	The home of the Duke and Duchess of Devonshire. It was built in 1555.	Bakewell, Derbyshire, DE45 1PP	www.chatsworth-houseshop.com
Hadrian's Wall	The most important monument built by the Romans in Britain. It is the best known frontier in the entire Roman Empire and stands as a reminder of past glories of one of the world's greatest civilisations. Designated a World Heritage Site in 1987, Hadrian's Wall ranks alongside the Taj Mahal and other treasures of the great wonders of the world. When it was built in stone, the wall was some 73 miles long and 5 metres high. It was one of the Roman Empire's greatest feats of engineering.	various	www.northumberland.gov.uk/VG/romans.html
Hampton Court Palace	State apartments, costumed guides, spectacular works of art, 60 acres of riverside gardens and 500 years of royal history.	Hampton Court Palace, East Molesey, Surrey, KT8 9AU	www.hrp.org.uk/webcode/hampton_home.asp
Stonehenge	Stonehenge is a prehistoric monument of unique importance, a World Heritage Site, surrounded by remains of ceremonial and domestic structures – some older than the monument itself.	Stonehenge, English Heritage, Nr Amesbury, SP4 7DE	www.english-heritage.org.uk
Tower of London	The Tower of London has been the setting for many great events during its 900-year history as a royal palace and fortress, prison and place of execution, arsenal, mint, menagerie and jewel house. The Tower is a World Heritage site.	HM Tower of London, London, EC3N 4AB	www.hrp.org.uk/webcode/tower_home.asp

FIND IT OUT

Look for the websites of English Heritage and the National Trust. Print out or make a list of the main work of these two organisations.

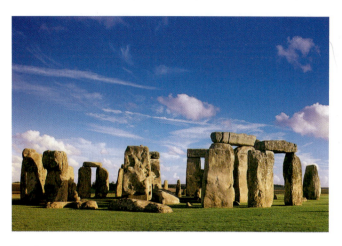
Stonehenge

Edinburgh Castle

Home-based leisure

The home-based activities that many of us enjoy are also a facility in the leisure industry. These are:

- reading;
- watching TV;
- listening to music or the radio;
- playing computer games;
- gardening;
- do-it-yourself;
- crafts like knitting and sewing.

FIND IT OUT

What we do at home in our leisure time often depends on our age. Ask all the members of your family how many hours a week they spend doing any of the above home-based activities. Put this information into a spreadsheet on your computer. What is the most popular home-based leisure activity in your home?

Changes in leisure activities

There have been changes over the past 20 years or so in the way we spend our leisure time:

- computer games are much more readily available and the number of households with a home computer has increased;
- many more households now have health and fitness equipment in their homes;
- the older activity of cycling has increased in popularity;

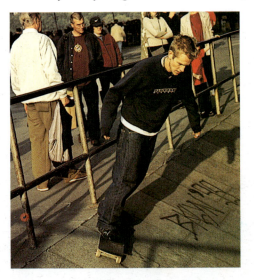

- skateboarding has become popular and many younger people now have skateboards and can use them close to their homes during their leisure time;
- many large do-it-yourself stores, such as Homebase and Focus DIY, have opened and have become a regular shopping trip for some members of the household. Their products are easily available to the general public and this has increased the amount of time people spend doing their own home improvements.

Products and services of the leisure industry

As well as providing the facility itself for customers to use, for example a leisure centre, the leisure industry also offers a number of other **products** or **services** to their customers. They offer these products and services to encourage their customers to come back to their organisation as well as to make more money.

A leisure centre would offer the following products and services to its customers:

- a range of different sports activities that customers can pay to take part in (service);
- lessons and classes for each of the different range of sports activities that customers can pay for if they wish to improve their performance (service);
- the use of the leisure centre for functions, such as weddings or birthday parties (service);

THE JARGON DRAGON

product – a product is a physical thing; it is something you pay for and can take away with you, for example a can of drink or a tennis racquet

service – this is a general term used to describe everything other than products that may be sold by an organisation (for example, the hire of a tennis court)

- machines in the foyer or reception area that customers can buy drinks and snacks from (products);
- a restaurant or coffee bar where customers can buy food and drinks (product);

THE JARGON DRAGON

discount – a reduced rate, meaning that a member would pay less than a non-member

hiring – paying by the hour or day for the use of equipment that belongs to a centre

- **discounts** to members or groups of people. For example, there may be a discount for groups of over 10 people who use the centre on a regular basis for **hiring** a badminton court (a service);
- discounts for members who buy sports equipment, such as trainers or running shoes from the leisure centre (a product and a service);
- the hiring of equipment for customers who cannot afford to buy their own (a service).

A hotel, on the other hand, as we will see later in this unit, might provide its customers with the following products and services:

- meals and accommodation;
- conference facilities – these are rooms that businesses can use when they are, for example, training their staff in a particular area. The conference facilities would be used by the business and the hotel would provide tables, chairs, paper, pens, refreshments and equipment, such as an overhead projector or computer for a slide show;
- banqueting facilities – these are facilities for large numbers of people to attend dinners and official functions; the hotel would organise the room(s), arrange the menus, waiters and waitresses and drinks;
- wedding receptions;
- dinner and dance evenings or weekends.

FIND IT OUT

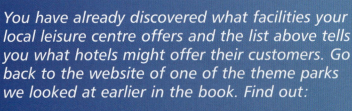

You have already discovered what facilities your local leisure centre offers and the list above tells you what hotels might offer their customers. Go back to the website of one of the theme parks we looked at earlier in the book. Find out:

1. *What products do they offer to their customers?*

2. *What services do they offer their customers?*

Now answer the same questions about one of the English Heritage sites that you looked at earlier.

Factors affecting how leisure time is spent

There are many different factors that affect the way we spend our leisure time. Some of these are:

- our age;
- our culture, which means where we come from and what we are used to doing;
- any special needs that we might have;
- whether we are spending our leisure time alone, with another person, or with our family;
- whether we are male or female;
- whether we are spending our leisure time with a group of people that we meet socially just to do the leisure activity;
- how easy it is to reach the leisure facility;
- how interested we are in doing the leisure activity;
- whether it is trendy to be doing the leisure activity;
- whether our family and friends approve of the leisure activity;
- how much it costs to do the leisure activity.

Let's take these reasons one by one.

Age group

Different age groups will have different needs and interests. Activities that are popular with younger people may not appeal to older ones. In the same way, those activities that appeal to the older generation may not appeal to those of your

generation. However, it is also possible that some of the older generation might be very good at one of the leisure activities usually thought to be for younger people. This could be because they have been doing it for a number of years and have become expert at it.

Think
IT THROUGH

Why might the older generation not be interested in some of the leisure activities carried out by you and your friends? Why do some of the things the older generation enjoy doing not appeal to you?

FIND IT OUT

Look at the list of leisure activities that we talked about earlier in this unit.

	Age group			
	12–18	18–35	35–50	50+
Reading				
Playing sport				
Watching sport				
Going to the cinema				
Going to a disco				
Walking				
Watching TV				
Listening to the radio				
Listening to music				
Eating out				
Playing computer games				
Visiting a tourist attraction				

> Now ask at least 10 people of different age groups which activities they like to do. Put a tick in the age group box beside each activity if they say they are interested.
>
> Are any of the activities popular with all age groups? If so, which ones are they and why do you think this might be the case?

Don't forget that something you liked to do in your leisure time five years ago may not be what you enjoy doing now. Some of your leisure activities nowadays you may not have heard about five years ago. Or you may not have been able to buy the equipment because you were not old enough or didn't have enough money.

> *Think about your favourite hobby or game you liked to play five years ago. Do you still have the same interests that you did then or have you moved onto another favourite hobby or game? Can you think why this might be?*

Think IT THROUGH

Culture

People's culture, which may include background or religion, can affect how they spend their leisure time. Some cultures and religions forbid drinking alcohol, so visits to a local pub to play darts or pool might not be a leisure activity they would choose. Some cultures have their own traditional forms of leisure activity, which may include dancing, singing or craftwork.

If leisure activities are influenced by culture this may mean that an area will have local facilities for this culture. Leisure activities that have not been popular in the area at any time, or for some years, will not be offered. For example, if tennis courts are not used in a public park then they tend to be grassed over. Or if a leisure centre does not attract enough local people then it faces the risk of being closed as local councils need to make sure they spend their money wisely on the local community.

Think
IT THROUGH

Are there any facilities in your area that have been closed down because of lack of support from the community? Can you think why this might have been the case?

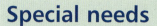

Special needs

It used to be the case that people with special needs, such as wheelchair users, the visually impaired and the hearing impaired, could not enjoy many leisure activities. Leisure centres and community centres, as well as stadiums and even libraries, did not have facilities for them. Many of these places did not have ramps for wheelchairs or specially trained staff to coach, teach or help those with special needs.

Most facilities now have these ways of encouraging people with special needs to become involved. There are now wheelchair basketball teams, visually impaired swimmers and people with special needs who regularly run marathons around the country. There is also the disabled Olympics in which people with a variety of special needs participate in their chosen sport.

FIND IT OUT

Choose a sport or leisure activity from those we have mentioned so far in this unit. Find out what special facilities there are for someone who has special needs. For instance, can those in a wheelchair attend classes to help them train for the sport or activity? Does the facility offer assistance to the hearing impaired or the visually impaired?

Type of household (families, single people, couples)

Households, particularly those with younger children, need to find leisure activities that would suit all the family. Families will look for leisure facilities that welcome children and cater especially for their needs. Many leisure centres and even some of the larger shops have crèches and specially trained staff to look after children while their parents enjoy their adult leisure activity. Many leisure centres offer family membership rates and some of the major tourist attractions and theme parks offer free or reduced prices for children under the age of five. Single parents will also take advantage of these facilities offered by various centres or attractions.

Go to the website of your local council and find their recreational division. Can you find out whether your local leisure centre offers family membership rates? Do they have a crèche or child-minding facilities?

Single people or couples who do not have children certainly have more freedom to choose when and where they enjoy their leisure. Some leisure facilities are only open to people who do not bring children at certain times of the day. This is particularly true of pubs, restaurants and discos.

Places offering leisure activities need to make sure that they can cope with both families with children and couples or single people without. They try to balance what both groups of people need and make each group as welcome as the other. By doing this they can make sure that all groups enjoy themselves and that the facility is popular.

Does your local swimming pool have adult-only swimming sessions? Try to find this out and also see if you can find out whether they have special sessions for people who are retired and for children. What times of the day apply to these special sessions? Is it true that adult-only sessions are often held during the day, when children are at school? When are the special sessions for children held?

Gender

In the past some sports and leisure activities used to be male or female only. Now this is not the case; there are women's football teams and rugby teams. Many men enjoy cooking or sewing, which used to be considered as just something that women did.

It is not always possible, particularly in sports, for men and women to compete against one another, but they can train and learn how to play a sport together. Many of the other leisure activities, such as gardening, playing computer games or watching TV now have little to do with gender and are enjoyed by nearly everyone.

Social groups

We often choose our leisure activities because friends, family or neighbours do them. At school you may often choose your leisure activity because a friend introduced you to it. Also at school you may not be able to do some sports or there may not be clubs after school for the leisure activity you enjoy. Having a favourite sport or leisure activity is a good way to make friends and if you like certain people and enjoy spending time with them then you are more likely to copy what they like to do.

Are there any leisure activities that you do because a friend, family member or neighbour introduced you to them? Would you have started this leisure activity if you hadn't had someone to go along with the first time?

Think
IT THROUGH

There are other things that influence what people choose to do in their leisure time, including:

- The availability of local facilities. If it is not easy to take part in a particular type of leisure activity, then this may often mean that people choose to do something else that is easier to do.

- The availability of transport. Complicated journeys or long distances to travel can often put people off from taking part in leisure activities. Once the travel time is added to the leisure activity itself, it may mean that too much time is taken up.

- Their interests. Something has to grab your interest before you would be likely to take part in an activity. It may be a TV programme that grabs your interest or a poster or magazine article, but if you are not interested, you are not likely to get involved. That is why most sports and other activities try to make themselves sound as exciting as possible.

- Fashion. Leisure activities are sometimes trendy only for a short period of time. Skateboarding, for example, was very popular in the 1970s but fell out of fashion until quite recently. Now there are skate shops and skate parks across the country again because it has become fashionable once more.

- The influence of family and friends. One of the major reasons people take up a leisure activity is because someone they know is already doing it, or perhaps wants to do it and needs someone to come along with them. Sometimes it has the opposite effect and if an older or younger brother or sister is really into something then this may put you off doing it yourself.

- How much money they have to spend on leisure. Not all leisure activities cost a lot of money, but many do, particularly when you are just starting out. If you wanted to join a local football team you would have to pay for the kit and your boots before they would even think of letting you play. Some other leisure activities can cost hundreds or thousands of pounds a year. Horse riding, for example, can start quite cheaply once you have bought the clothes, as you can hire a horse and tuition by the hour, but once you become more seriously involved with the activity and want to buy and stable your own horse, you would need several thousand pounds and several hundred each year to keep your leisure activity going.

Laura didn't like having to get on a bus in the dark but she had no choice. If she wanted to learn how to swim and get her lifesaving certificate she would have to make the 10 mile round trip at least three times a week. She'd been told by one of the teachers at school and by her aunt that she had a real talent and that she should keep her interests going, whatever it took.

Stuart used to like football and he was quite good at it. He used to play in goal, but he didn't think it was trendy any more and he took up skateboarding. The trouble was that it was more expensive and he had to do a paper round and a Saturday job just to pay for the equipment he needed. His parents told him he was mad to spend £100 on a skateboard but his friends thought the new board was really cool.

Look at the bullet list of influences before the case study and then answer the following questions:

Q1 *Which two reasons on the list had an influence on what Laura does as her leisure activity?*

Q2 *Why did Stuart change his sport and what other two reasons from the list relate to Stuart's story?*

Employment opportunities in the leisure industry

There are many different jobs available within the leisure industry. Those detailed below are not the only jobs offered but are examples of the kind of work available.

Think
IT THROUGH

List the jobs in the leisure industry that you would be interested in applying for at present, should they become available.

Now try to answer the following questions as honestly as possible. This may help you understand the types of things to think about when choosing what jobs to apply for.

1 *Do you prefer to work by yourself or as a member of a group?*

2 *Do you like working indoors or outdoors?*

3 *Do you like working with computers or other equipment?*

4 *Do you like working with numbers?*

5 *Do you like writing?*

6 *Do you like talking to people?*

7 *Do you like drawing and designing things?*

8 *Do you arrive at school on time?*

9 *Do you get bored easily?*

10 *Do you mind dressing formally?*

11 *Do you like studying?*

12 *Do you know what your main strengths are?*

13 *Do you know what your main weaknesses are?*

14 *Do you know where you would like to be in 5 years' time?*

15 *Do you have an ambition for your future?*

Leisure assistants

A leisure assistant would be expected to be able to turn their hands to almost anything in the leisure industry. As you can see from the two jobs advertised, the job involves 'general duties', which is a way of saying that almost anything that needs to be done will be given to a leisure assistant. It is not the most glamorous job in the leisure industry but it is often a good starting point and a way to learn what is involved.

Casual leisure assistant

To work up to 20 hours per week at £4.00 per hour. Leisure assistant required to help with the general duties including setting up of equipment, cleaning and activity supervision.

Sports assistants or leisure assistants

Leisure Centre currently has two vacancies for sports assistants or leisure assistants. We are looking for customer-focused individuals to carry out a range of duties from lifeguarding to the setting up of sports equipment. Ideally you will hold a recognised lifesaving qualification or will be willing to work towards gaining one. Previous experience in a sport-related environment is desirable but not essential. Please see the two rotas below.

Post no. 1
Week 1: Tue 17.30–23.30, Thu 17.30–23.30, weekend off.
Week 2: Tue 17.30–23.30, Sat 08.45–14.15, Sun 09.00–16.30.
Week 3: Tue 17.30–23.30, Fri 17.30– 23.30, Sat 14.15– 21.30, Sun 16.15–23.00.

Post no. 2
Week 1: Wed 17.30–23.30, Fri 17.30–23.30, Sat 14.15–19.00, Sun 16.15–23.00.
Week 2: Wed 17.30–23.30, Thur 17.30–23.30, weekend off.
Week 3: Wed 17.30–23.30, Sat 08.45–14.15, Sun 09.00–16.30.

We offer attractive benefits including generous annual leave, free use of our fitness and pool facilities and a commitment to the training and development of our staff.
Salary: £4.20 up to £5.77 per hour.

Fitness instructors

Some of the top fitness instructors in the country earn large amounts of money but every leisure centre will have fitness instructors who will run classes for those who want to become a bit fitter and, perhaps, lose some weight. You would need to be quite well trained to become a fitness instructor. There are plenty of jobs around, particularly in private health clubs, which always need new ways for their customers to keep fit but, of course, the instructor has to be super-fit!

As you can see from the **job description** for a fitness instructor, they have many added responsibilities.

THE JARGON DRAGON

job description – this explains what the job involves and is useful for matching the right person to that job

Fitness instructor
Leading operator requires an outstanding fitness professional to work in one of its most exclusive clubs. Excellent career opportunities await those with an outgoing personality and relevant qualifications.

Salary: £13 000 a year.

JOB TITLE: FITNESS INSTRUCTOR

REPORTING TO: FITNESS SUPERVISOR

JOB PURPOSE: To provide exercise prescription, encouragement, support and advice to members in order to assist them in achieving their fitness goals.

KEY RESPONSIBILITIES:

FINANCE
To promote member uptake of personal training and other promotions.
To reduce freelance instructor costs by teaching studio classes as and when required and where qualified.

OPERATIONS
- To perform a high level of instruction in all areas.
- To carry out lifestyle profiles and fitness assessments.
- To patrol the gym, correcting exercise technique and offering assistance to members.
- To ensure that the gymnasium and its equipment are clean and tidy at all times.
- To keep up to date with changes and developments in fitness principles.

MEMBERS
- To ensure that all members receive the highest standards of customer service.
- To follow up members and regularly update their exercise programme.
- To gain an understanding of all departments and their operations.

PEOPLE
- To communicate effectively with all other departments.
- To attend weekly team meetings and training sessions.
- To understand and adhere to the health and safety and equal opportunities policies.

Carry out any other reasonable request as directed by the fitness supervisor.

REQUIREMENTS:
Relevant fitness qualifications (minimum NVQ Level 2).
Excellent communication skills.
A firm understanding of excellence in customer service.
The ability to motivate and train members to achieve their fitness goals.

Lifeguards

By law, every swimming pool or anywhere that the general public swims, like a lake or even a beach, needs to have a lifeguard. Aside from being a strong swimmer, a lifeguard would also have to know the basics of first aid and be able to handle situations when people find themselves in difficulties when swimming.

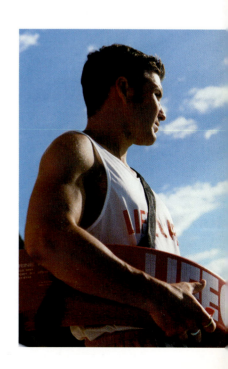

Lifeguard
Salary £3.70 – £4.20/hr
Responsible for lifeguarding the swimming pools during peak times, carrying out regular pool water tests, ensuring the pool areas are kept in a clean condition and maintaining the general cleanliness of the changing rooms and other areas of the club as specified.

Qualifications/experience: a current lifeguard qualification.

JOB TITLE: LIFEGUARD

REPORTING TO: DUTY MANAGER

JOB PURPOSE: To ensure the safety of all swimming pool users whilst delivering the highest standards of customer service.

KEY RESPONSIBILITIES:

FINANCE

- To promote member uptake of swimming lessons and other promotions.
- To ensure cost effective use of all material and equipment used in the swimming pool.

OPERATIONS

- To patrol the swimming pool and ensure the safety of all users.
- To assist with pool water testing as and when required.
- To assist with attendant, reception and, where qualified, fitness duties.
- To set up and take down any equipment needed in the swimming pool for specialist activities.

MEMBERS

- To gain an understanding of all departments and their operations.
- To ensure that all members receive the highest standards of customer service.

PEOPLE

- To communicate effectively with all other departments.
- To attend meetings and training sessions on a regular basis.
- To understand and adhere to the health-and-safety and equal opportunities policies.
- To communicate effectively with all other departments.
- Carry out any other reasonable request as directed by the duty manager.

REQUIREMENTS:

- Nationally recognised lifeguard qualification.
- A firm understanding of excellence in customer service.
- Excellent communication skills.

See if you can find out how to obtain a nationally recognised lifeguard qualification. Do you know someone who has this qualification? If not, you could try your school or local library first. Maybe your local swimming pool offers lessons?

FIND IT OUT

Ground staff

Ground staff are some of the most important people to work at various football, cricket, rugby and hockey grounds and on golf courses. These are the people who make sure that the grass and the pitches or courses are in good condition for people to be able to use them for their sports. The term 'ground staff' also refers to almost anyone who works in a stadium and has something to do with parking, safety and seating.

Ground staff also work in parks and make sure that the grass, plants and trees are being cared for and that any necessary gardening work is carried out. Very often they report to park rangers.

Park wardens

As you can see from the job description, a park warden's job is very varied. It involves managing parks on a day-to-day basis. They deal with safety, litter and damage and carry out regular patrols to make sure that the park is not being vandalised or misused.

Park warden

The warden service operates with four wardens, each covering a different area of the borough, 365 days of the year, with their rounds and daily hours varying according to the season – with longer hours covering peak periods of demand, such as in the summer.

We currently have four park wardens to provide all-year maintenance for the parks, sports pitches and green spaces in the borough.

Park visits

Regular visits are scheduled to every green amenity in the borough to ensure that our local parks and the facilities in them are kept in good condition. These visits help us to make sure that play areas are safe for children to use and that litter bins are being regularly emptied. Park visits also help to control litter and dog fouling in the borough.

The park wardens' work

- Playground inspections (over 2500 per year).
- Control of outdoor sports facilities.
- Locking and unlocking and community patrols of parks and cemeteries.
- Minor repairs to parks furniture.
- Response to litter complaints.
- Customer queries and requests both directly and through the council's recreation and amenities officers.

Play area inspections

Regular inspections are carried out by the park wardens to ensure that all of our children's play areas are clean, that park bins are emptied, and that fences and gates are secure. Regular checks are also carried out by the wardens to make sure that the furniture and play equipment at each site is safe and free from defects. Park wardens also check that sports facilities are in good condition and meet our quality standards.

Park hygiene

Park wardens manage the hygiene standards in parks and green facilities. Wardens check that litter and dog bins are kept in a good condition and are being regularly emptied, they monitor the levels of littering and dog fouling, and work to ensure that our area is kept clean and safe for local residents and visitors.

Restaurant managers

Restaurant managers may not actually have to know very much about cooking as their job is to manage the staff who prepare, cook and serve the food and drinks to the customers. A restaurant manager would be expected to deal with any day-to-day problems, handle complaints, supervise the waiters, waitresses and whoever deals with money. It is therefore important that he or she has good communication skills. This is also important because the restaurant manager is the one who deals with the customers the most.

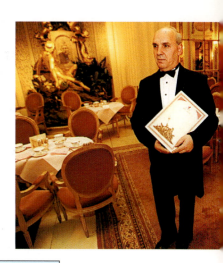

Assistant restaurant manager

Have you the experience we are looking for? You should have assisted in the day-to-day running of a fine dining restaurant and you need a pleasant attitude towards both your customers and your colleagues. You must be hard working and have the ability to work well under pressure. References are essential and will be verified. Short-term live-in accommodation may be an option; however senior staff are encouraged to seek accommodation outside the hotel. To apply, all you have to do is send us your CV today.

Role or area: hotel/catering.

Term type: permanent.

Location: Berkshire.

Salary: £13 000 – £13 500 p.a.

As we have already mentioned, there are hundreds of different types of jobs in the leisure industry. Visit the following two website and search for jobs that you will find under hospitality, tourism or leisure.

www.jobsearch.co.uk

www.monster.co.uk

Can you find any jobs in the industry for which you could apply?

FIND IT OUT

The travel and tourism industry

The travel and tourism industry helps us to do what we want to do with our leisure time. Without the services provided by travel and tourism we would not be able to visit some of the visitor attractions and historic sites we have already discussed.

Tourism is a broad area to explain but the best way to remember what it really covers is that it is related to temporary absence from home. In other words, even if you stay in a hotel for one night, either for pleasure or for work, then you have entered into the tourism industry.

The main reasons why people use the tourism industry are:

- to go on holiday;
- to go on a sightseeing trip;
- to visit one of the visitor attractions that we have already discussed;
- to visit friends;
- to visit relatives;
- to play in a sports event;
- to watch a sports event;
- for health reasons;
- for educational purposes;
- for business.

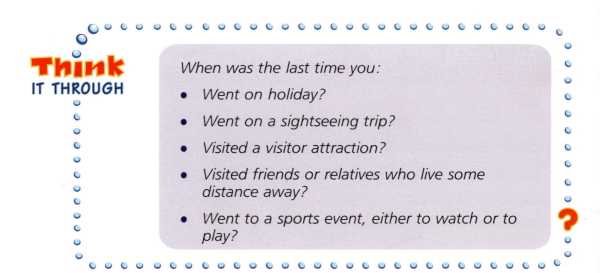

Think IT THROUGH

When was the last time you:
- *Went on holiday?*
- *Went on a sightseeing trip?*
- *Visited a visitor attraction?*
- *Visited friends or relatives who live some distance away?*
- *Went to a sports event, either to watch or to play?*

A holiday

Holidays come in all shapes and sizes and prices. As we will see later, holidays can just mean staying at a hotel or a bed and breakfast guesthouse and then visiting an attraction or sightseeing. Some holidays may include the cost of the travel and the accommodation. Once you are there, you would have to buy your own food. Other holidays, called 'all-inclusive', mean that once you have paid for the holiday everything you eat and drink is included in the price. Holidays, of course, tend to be taken by most people during the school holiday periods, such as Easter or the summer break.

Ask your classmates where they have been on holiday in the United Kingdom. When you've asked everyone, find out if there is one area of the United Kingdom that is the most popular. Now ask them if they have ever visited another country on holiday. Is there one other country that more people have visited than others?

FIND IT OUT

Sightseeing

Sometimes, in order to have a good look around one particular town, city, or part of the country, it is necessary to stay overnight. Sightseeing usually involves taking a quick trip around all of the major sites in a particular city. In most of the bigger cities open-topped buses are available with a commentary that shows you all of the major tourist sites and places of interest. Sometimes it is impossible to see everything that there is to see in one day, so sightseeing trips need to be well planned so that you can see as much as possible in the time that you have available to you.

Visiting an attraction

There are thousands of different attractions up and down the country, from zoos and museums to historic buildings and theme parks. Some attractions are only temporary, as they may be special shows put on for the public, such as air shows or parades.

Sometimes visiting an attraction means that you will need to stay in accommodation overnight so that you can spend as long a time as possible at the attraction without having to travel too far each day.

Visiting friends or relatives

Visiting friends or relatives, either by car, coach, rail or even air, can be a holiday in itself. If friends or family live in a very different part of the country, you will have the opportunity to enjoy all of the local attractions and sites that they see on a daily basis. The only real difference is that you may be staying with the friends or family and will not require accommodation that you have to pay for. This doesn't stop you from being a tourist.

> *If friends or relatives came to stay with you, where would you take them for a day out?*

Going to a sports event as a spectator or to participate

Hundreds of thousands of people go to sporting events every week. The most popular, of course, is football, where some of the larger clubs can accommodate over 60 000 people at a time. If you are a spectator, that means you are just going to watch and it will mean that you will have to travel to the venue, pay to get in and probably buy food, drink or a souvenir while you are there.

If you are participating in an event, then you will still have to get there, but the organisers may have arranged travel and accommodation for you. Many thousands of people are involved in amateur sports and recreation. If you were in a local football team, for example, your club would arrange a coach or a minibus to take you to the match.

Business

Business travel is an extremely important part of the travel and tourism industry. Thousands of people take business trips every week. They may be visiting customers or their **suppliers**, attending meetings or special events to do with their work. Some travel agents specialise in business travel and aim to get their business customers to where they want to go in the most efficient way.

Business travellers look for good value for money for their trip and would expect a high level of service and a good place to spend an overnight visit if they need it. Businessmen and women who travel on a regular basis as part of their job often receive discounts for frequent journeys.

THE JARGON DRAGON

supplier – an organisation that provides the business with the items or service it needs, for example, printer paper

Are there any travel agents in your local area that specialise in business travel? They will often include this in their advertisements, either on the Internet or in the Yellow Pages. What do they offer the business traveller?

The key components of the travel and tourism industry

The travel and tourism industry is made up of many different organisations, all of which have their own part to play in helping individuals and businesses to make their plans for travel.

Travel agents

Even the smallest of travel agencies will be able to offer you a range of holiday information. Travel agents arrange the details of a trip for people and they make their money from the tour operators that they book holidays with. They have a variety of different brochures from the tour operators to assist customers. They also have access to a great deal of information about travel and accommodation via their computer terminals or reservation systems. We look at these computer-based systems a little later in this unit.

You would use the services of a travel agent if you wanted to book any of the following:

- A package holiday – where the flight and accommodation are included in the price you pay. A package holiday could be within the United Kingdom or to an overseas country. The travel agent is able to give information about the holidays offered by a number of different tour operators.

- A flight only – where the travel agent books the flight for you but you arrange your own accommodation. Again, this could be a flight within the United Kingdom or one to another country.

- Accommodation only – perhaps you are driving to your holiday and only need the travel agent to book your hotel or guesthouse.
- Rail travel – you can book train tickets at the travel agency.
- Rail travel and accommodation – another form of package holiday, where everything is booked for you.
- Theatre, concert and event tickets – sometimes this is a form of package as the cost of the coach trip is included in the price you pay the travel agent.
- Coach travel – you can book coach tickets at the travel agency.
- Coach travel and accommodation – another form of package holiday, where everything is booked for you.
- Car service to and from airports and ferry ports. It can be expensive to park at airports and ferry ports and sometimes it is cheaper and more convenient to book a car to take you there and collect you when you return.
- Information about passports and advice on the **visa** requirements of different countries.
- Information and advice about the injections a visitor may need before visiting a particular country. This is particularly important when visiting countries that have diseases that are not common in the United Kingdom, such as cholera, tuberculosis and typhoid.
- Information and advice about specific areas of the country and of the world. Many travel agencies send their staff to visit the different countries and resorts so that they can give correct information to their customers.

THE JARGON DRAGON

visa – some countries require visitors to have a visa as well as a passport; a visa is a document that gives the visitor permission to enter the country for a limited length of time

What injections would you need to go to the following places?

- *South Africa;*
- *India;*
- *Jamaica.*

You could ask any travel agent in your local area or you could see if you could find out yourself on the Internet.

FIND IT OUT

Tour operators

Holiday tour operators have offices that operate a lot like travel agencies. The only major difference is that you can only buy holidays from the range that they offer, so you don't have the choice of different companies that you find in a travel agency. Tour operators exist in local, regional, national and international areas.

The names on the front of holiday brochures are usually those of the tour operators. These are the organisations that have put together the holidays shown in the brochure and had the brochure printed. Europe has the largest tour operators; some, like Thomson, sell as many as 3 million package holidays per year. There are three different types of tour operators. These are:

- The *inbound* tour operator, which provides services for visitors to the United Kingdom.
- The *outbound* tour operator, which provides services for United Kingdom residents who wish to travel abroad.
- The *domestic* tour operator, which provides services for United Kingdom residents visiting other parts of the United Kingdom (including Northern Ireland, the Isle of Man and the Isle of Wight).

FIND IT OUT

Travel agents and tour operators have to be registered with an organisation called ABTA. Find out what the initials stand for and what the organisation does to help the general public.

Tourist information

Tourist information centres (TICs) are an important part of a local area's ability to provide accurate information to visitors. They do this from their offices by supplying leaflets, brochures and other forms of information. This is not just about the area in which their offices are situated but about the rest of the region. The TICs can arrange local and regional tours for visitors. They can also offer:

- local bed-booking services – they will make reservations for you at a local hotel or guesthouse;

- book-a-bed-ahead services – they will telephone a TIC in another area and book a bed at your next destination. This is ideal for anyone touring around the country.

Tourist information centres are very popular and deal with 10 million enquiries throughout the country every year.

If possible visit your local tourist information centre and briefly note down what information it supplies to tourists visiting the area. If this is not possible, use the Internet to find the tourist information centre in either Chester, York or Portsmouth. Briefly note what information it has for tourists.

FIND IT OUT

Guiding services

Some coach companies and other organisations offer local, regional, national and international guide services. Often the coach will have a representative of the company on board to talk to the passengers about the area through which they are travelling. They would also guide the passengers on the different stops they make and give them information about the history of the place they are visiting. Very often this could be an historic building and the guide would accompany the visitors on the tour, pointing out anything of particular interest on the way.

Guiding services are not available in all areas of the United Kingdom, but are usually found in areas that have specific attractions. Areas that have an interesting historical background, or are associated with celebrities or famous people

(such as the Jack the Ripper tours in the East End of London) will have a variety of guiding services available through the local council or local bus and coach operators.

> Search on the Internet using the word 'Shakespeare' and see if you can find a guiding service which could show you all of the main sites associated with this famous writer in Stratford-upon-Avon.

Online travel services

The growth of the Internet has meant that many businesses, no matter how small they are, have their own website. Some of these website allow customers to research a holiday, finding out about the resort, prices and the different ways of getting there. Customers can then book their holidays online without needing to go to a travel agent. They receive an email to confirm their booking, with further information as to when tickets will be received. The tickets and any other information would be posted to the customer as normal.

Travel agents also make use of online services. This helps them to find a choice of flights, holidays or accommodation from different tour operators and airlines to match their customer requests. They often do this while the customer is in their office and the booking can be made immediately if the customer likes one of the options.

> You can see how easy it is to research a holiday by going to www.aito.co.uk.
>
> Pretend you want to go on holiday to South America and you want an adventure holiday. How many different options can you find? Write a list of the brochures that they suggest you should get.
>
> As you will see this website gives you a lot of options. You could investigate the choices they have with a country of your own choice.

Accommodation

The United Kingdom has a huge variety of accommodation available to travellers. There are around 50 000 hotels, guest houses and bed and breakfast places in the country, of which 40 000 have less than 10 rooms each. These generally fall into the following main categories.

- *Hotels* are basically overnight, furnished and serviced bedrooms. The standard of accommodation varies but, at the very least, they all have a bed, wardrobe and table and chair. Some may only have a handful of bedrooms, whereas others, such as the larger and more expensive London hotels, have hundreds of rooms and a staff of 600 or more. The services provided are the cleaning of the bedroom and bathroom and often tea- and coffee-making facilities plus a television.

Search the Internet using the words 'London Hotels'. You will find hundreds of website. Choose at least three and compare the prices for each night you could stay in the hotels. What do you get for your money?

FIND IT OUT

- *Motels* – are usually conveniently situated alongside major transport routes. They tend to offer fairly basic facilities and are there to provide the opportunity for the traveller to break the journey. Some often have the same facilities as a hotel.
- *Guesthouses* are a cheaper alternative to hotels. They are usually smaller than the average hotel and only have a small number of rooms. Sometimes these are in people's homes and the accommodation is offered on a bed-and-breakfast or room-only basis. The rooms will often be basic but pleasant and homely and some have televisions and tea- and coffee-making facilities.
- *Holiday homes* are houses, flats and even villas or boats that customers can rent out for a weekend, a week or any number of weeks. You have the home to yourself, with all the things that you would expect to find in a house, including furniture, kitchen equipment and televisions.

Go to the website of Hoseasons at www.hoseasons.co.uk. They rent out houses, lodges and boats. How much would it cost to rent a house in Norfolk for a week for a family of two adults and two children? What facilities or attractions are near the house?

- *Holiday villages* are groups of holiday homes (either chalets or caravans). Customers can choose whether they want to cook for themselves or eat in the restaurants of the village. They usually have the same services as a hotel and many facilities that the customers can use in the village, such as children's playgrounds, and perhaps swimming pools.

Butlins, Pontin's and Center Parcs are all examples of businesses that offer holiday villages for customers. Go to www.butlins.co.uk and find out where they have holiday villages or camps. How much would it cost to stay for a week for a family of two adults and two children in Minehead in June? Now find Center Parcs' website and compare their prices to those of Butlins. Does Center Parcs offer more facilities than Butlins?

- *Tents* – many people choose to take their own tents to campsites for which they pay a rent for every night they stay. Some of the larger campsites have their own static tents and customers can book them in advance. Larger campsites have similar facilities to caravan sites.

- *Youth hostels* have rooms of varying sizes, from two-bedded rooms to larger dormitory-style accommodation. Many have shared bathrooms, although en-suite facilities are available. Almost all youth hostels have kitchens for guests to prepare and cook their own food, while many of the larger ones also have restaurants where meals can be bought. In the past, guests were asked to do chores, but this is no longer required of them.

Go to www.yha.org.uk, which is the website of the Youth Hostelling Association of England and Wales. Answer the following questions:

1. What do you have to do to become a member of the YHA?
2. How many youth hostels are there in the south-west of England?
3. How much would it cost for two adults and two children to stay one night at the Broad Haven Hostel at Haverfordwest in Pembrokeshire?

Catering

As we have seen, there are several options of where to stay when travelling, but there is also the question of what to eat and when to eat it while we are away. The catering options are:

- *Self-catering* – which means your accommodation will have kitchen facilities. You would choose either to cook for yourself or go out to a pub or restaurant to eat.
- *Continental breakfast* – which means your hotel or guesthouse provides you with the room plus a roll or pastry, fruit juice, yoghurt, coffee and/or tea. Sometimes this breakfast is taken in the room or often in the dining room of the accommodation.
- *Full English breakfast* – which means you are paying for the room plus a cooked breakfast, as well as cereal, toast, tea and/or coffee.

- *Half board* – which means in addition to the room and one of the breakfast options, the price you pay includes one more meal – either lunch or an evening meal.
- *Full board* – which means in addition to the room and one of the breakfast options, the price you pay includes lunch and an evening meal.

Attractions

As we have already seen, attractions can range from castles to zoos and from theatres to mountains. The travel and tourism industry works alongside the leisure industry in aiming to give customers ways of getting to these attractions. They provide places for them to stay once they are there and food and other facilities that they can enjoy during the visit.

Around the attractions in the United Kingdom, and in the rest of the world, the travel and tourism industry has built up the following facilities:

- transport links (air, road, sea and rail);
- accommodation links (hotels, guesthouses, self-catering, camping and caravan sites and youth hostels);
- catering links (restaurants, takeaways, snack bars and pubs);
- information services (tourist information centres, guide services, printed leaflets, maps and brochures);
- other attractions – because people are travelling to a particular area to see a major attraction, other, smaller or similar attractions may be set up to encourage the customer to stay longer and to enjoy themselves all the more.

Transportation

As we will shortly see, transportation is a very important part of the travel and tourism industry. After all, it is not enough to have the most exciting attraction or the most beautiful countryside if there is no way to get there. Transportation, the final component of the travel and tourism industry, is provided by a mixture of different organisations and businesses:

- Roads – for cars, buses and coaches – which are built by the government and local councils. Most major attractions have major roads close by.

- Buses and coaches, which are supplied mainly by private business and some councils.
- Airports, which are usually built by private businesses and used by private airlines to transport travellers over short or long distances.
- Ports, which are usually privately owned and are used by the various shipping businesses to transport travellers by sea to their destinations.
- Railways, which are now privately owned and are used to link various parts of the country. Most major attractions have railway stations close by and may provide buses and coaches to transport visitors from the railway station to the attraction.

Look at the website at www.alton-towers.co.uk and print out an area map of Alton Towers.

1. Find out how many miles Alton Towers is from London, Glasgow and Portsmouth.
2. Plan a journey from your location to Alton Towers by road.
3. Plan a journey from your location to Alton Towers by rail.

Different types of holidays

We already know some of the things that affect the way we spend our leisure time, including our age, our gender and how much money we have. As going on holiday is probably one of the most important ways in which we spend days or even weeks of our leisure time, it makes sense that these reasons remain the same. People of different age groups like different holidays, people from different cultures take different holidays and what our friends and family like affects where we go.

Package holidays

Package holidays are one of the most popular forms of holiday to destinations outside the United Kingdom. They are a very convenient way of travelling abroad because they include:

- the cost of all travel to and from the holiday destination;
- the cost of any airport duties and taxes;
- the cost of all accommodation at the destination;
- the cost of getting to the accommodation from the airport and the cost of the return journey to the airport at the end of the holiday.

A package holiday is an all-in-one product because the customer does not have to worry about any aspect of the holiday except, perhaps, **travel insurance**.

A package holiday would always include travel and accommodation, but could also include catering by one of the following:

- self-catering basis;
- bed-and-breakfast basis;
- half-board basis;
- full-board basis.

Some package holidays offer more than those given above. They sometimes offer the customer some or all of the following:

- All-inclusive holidays – where everything is included in the price you pay. This might include all meals and drinks taken during the holiday. This type of holiday has been popular for a number of years on sea cruises around, for example, the Caribbean, Mediterranean and the Far East. It is also now becoming more popular in larger hotels in Spain, Greece and other well-known holiday destinations.
- Car hire included in the price paid. Some package holidays are known as fly-drive holidays and the car is at the airport on arrival and can be used by the customer throughout their holiday. Often these types of package holiday are offered to visitors to America or Australia, where one of the popular ways of holidaying is to travel around the country from place to place.
- Days out are included in the price paid. Some package holidays include full- or half-day excursions to other parts of the area that is being visited. These excursions are often taken by coach.

THE JARGON DRAGON

travel insurance – this is paid by the customer to an insurance company. The travel insurance protects the customer in case of a problem with their holiday, or as a result of their holiday. Such a problem might be loss of suitcases, cancelled flight or illness while away.

- Children go free – some travel companies try to make their package holidays more interesting to families by offering free places to one child (or sometimes more) – for example, to those under the age of 10 or 12 who share accommodation with two adults.

Package holidays are usually booked by the customer through travel agents or directly through the tour operator, often either by telephone or by booking online. Many families search through many different brochures before they finally decide where to go on holiday.

Collect the travel brochures from at least three tour operators. Look at the package holidays to Corfu (a Greek island) in the last two weeks of July. What are the options for two adults and two children? Do any of your tour operators offer free places for children? What would the total cost of the holiday be for the two weeks if they went on a self-catering basis?

FIND IT OUT

The Package Travel, Package Holidays and Package Tours Regulations, 1992

These European Community Regulations came into force in 1992 and, usefully, they describe exactly what a package holiday should consist of:

'Package means the pre-arranged combination of at least two of the following components when sold or offered for sale at an inclusive price and when the service covers a period of more than twenty-four hours or includes overnight accommodation:

- transport
- accommodation
- other tourist services not ancillary to transport or accommodation and accounting for a significant proportion of the package.'

Independent travel

Some people prefer not to go abroad on a package holiday. Often they think that they can see more of the area they are visiting by travelling independently. This does not always mean that they travel alone but it does mean that they can have more choice about what flights they take, where they stay and how long they stay there. This type of travel is more popular with single people and couples who do not have children.

Those who intend to take an independent trip abroad have to do the following:

- Arrange their own travel by booking their flight, ferry crossing or coach travel directly with the airline, ferry, rail or coach companies. They could do this either by visiting the office, by telephone, or by booking online.
- Arrange their accommodation. They may have visited the area before and have contacts in a number of different places. However, if they have never been to their chosen destination before, then they could search the Internet for accommodation. Some people choose not to book their accommodation from the United Kingdom but wait until they arrive in their chosen area and find somewhere to sleep then.
- They have a good guidebook or some way of finding their way around their holiday destination, for example maps of the area.

FIND IT OUT

Pretend that you wanted to explore the island of Crete (Greece). Go to www.cheapflights.com. On their home page you will see the alphabet at the top of the screen. Click on H (for Heraklion, the airport town of Crete), then click on Heraklion on the next page. Choose the airports nearest to your home town. You should now find a list of the different airlines and some tour operators with whom you could book an independent flight to Heraklion. Go to the website of at least three different companies and compare the following:

1. The number of flights available on 22 July for one person.
2. The cost of the flight.
3. The departure and arrival times of the flight (what time does it leave the United Kingdom airport and what time does it get back into the United Kingdom after the holiday?).
4. Can you book online or do they give you a telephone number to contact?

Now go back to the www.cheapflights.com home page. There is a link to www.cheapnights.com. Click on 'more worldwide destinations' and click on the H (for Heraklion) at the top of the next page. Select Heraklion from the following page. Now answer the following questions:

1. How many hotels are there that an independent traveller could choose in Heraklion?
2. What is the temperature in Heraklion today?
3. Can you book online or do you have to make a telephone call to Greece?

Holidays involving short-haul and long-haul flights

Holidays abroad are often referred to in one of two different ways, short haul or long haul. These terms refer to the length of the flights involved in getting to the holiday destination.

Short-haul flights tend to be those that last for around four hours or a little more. Typical short-haul flights go to countries within Europe, for example Greece, Spain and Italy. As Europe is a very popular holiday destination for those choosing a package holiday, it is often the case that package holidays involve short-haul flights.

Long-haul flights are those that take more than seven hours; usually from the UK to another continent. Flights to Australia, for instance, often involve a stop in places like Singapore or Hong Kong, as they can take more than 15 hours in the air.

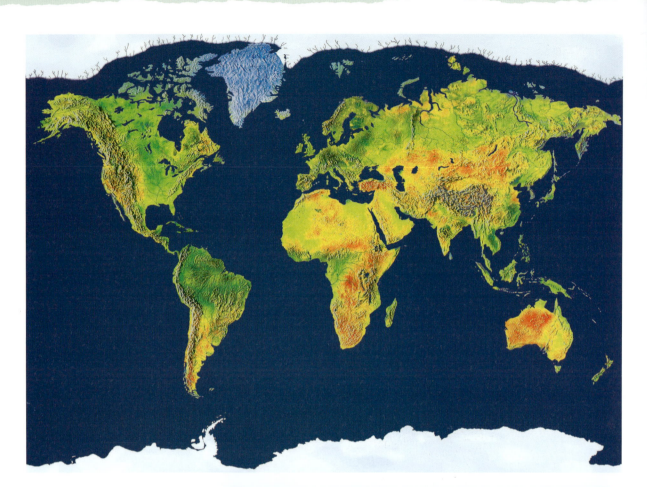

FIND IT OUT

Look at a map of the world. Write down at least three other countries that you could visit on holiday from the United Kingdom that would involve a long-haul flight.

Inbound and outbound holidays

Inbound holidays refer to holidays which are taken by overseas visitors coming to the UK, such as North American tourists flying across the Atlantic, or European tourists visiting the UK by ferry, a short-haul flight, or through the Eurotunnel by Eurostar.

Outbound holidays refer to all trips made abroad by UK residents, which include long flights to North America or Australia and shorter flights to other European cities. They can also include ferry trips across the Channel to France, Belgium or Holland, and shorter journeys to Scandinavia, such as Norway, Denmark or Sweden.

Domestic holidays

Holidays within the United Kingdom are still very popular. There are a number of advantages to enjoying your holiday here. These are:

- they are often cheaper;
- there are no language difficulties;
- money does not need to be changed into another currency;
- it probably will not be necessary to hire a car because you can take your own;
- it is usually a shorter travelling time to the destination.

There are, however, some disadvantages, including:

- unreliable weather – you are much more likely to see the sun in Spain in July than you are in the United Kingdom;
- not so much opportunity to experience new cultures or food from another country;
- holidays often have to be taken during school holidays, when United Kingdom resorts and attractions are busy and the roads are clogged with traffic.

You can use any of the accommodation and catering facilities we have talked about when you holiday in the United Kingdom. There are hundreds of guesthouses, hotels, chalets, caravan and camp sites in every part of the country.

Think IT THROUGH

Can you think of at least six destinations within the United Kingdom that are popular with domestic holidaymakers? Write them down and see how many of your classmates have ever visited one, or maybe all of them. What is the main attraction of each destination? Is it the sea, the mountains or the history behind the destination?

Special interest holidays

Sometimes holidays can be taken for a completely different reason than sightseeing or visiting attractions. There are holidays offered during which you can learn how to play golf, cook or scuba dive. Special interest holidays may focus on bird watching, walking or rambling, visiting vineyards or touring historic sites.

There are now hundreds of specialist tour operators offering special interest holidays as package holidays. Just like a normal package tour, they will arrange all of the travel and accommodation, as well as laying on the facilities that you would need to enjoy your special interest.

You can take a special interest domestic holiday or you can go to another country to learn to do something in which you are interested.

FIND IT OUT

Go to www.travelux.co.uk/specint.htm or www.travelword.co.uk/interest.htm and see if there are any special interest holidays available that you would like to go on. If you find one write down what you need to do to book a holiday like this.

Short breaks

Rome

Short break holidays are very popular as they give people the opportunity to go away just for a few days. Short breaks can be taken in the United Kingdom or abroad, particularly in a capital city of another European country. The important thing to remember is that the travel time needs to be short so that the time that you have for your short break is not eaten up by sitting in a car, coach, plane or train.

Many tour operators offer weekend breaks and mid-week breaks and these are ideal for people to be able to visit a city that they have never been to before and enjoy a taste of the culture and food in a relaxed atmosphere.

The four main travel methods, or modes of travel as they are sometimes known, are air, sea, road and rail.

Go to www.tvtravelshop.com and find the cheapest weekend break for two people in Paris. What is and what is not included in the package? What hotel would you be staying at? What information about Paris can you print from this website?

FIND IT OUT

Methods of travel

Air travel

Air travel is very fast and reliable. There are really only a few things that can affect air travel – bad weather conditions, strikes by airport workers or problems in a country over which the flight has to pass, such as a war or bad weather conditions.

For holidaymakers, two main types of flight can be used:

- *Charter flights*, which are used by tour operators to fly their package holiday customers to their destination. Very often independent travellers can also book seats on these charter flights, particularly if they are travelling at a time when the planes are not likely to be full.
- *Scheduled flights*, which are timetabled and will fly whether the plane is half full, full or nearly empty. These are more expensive than charter flights.

Major international airports in the United Kingdom

The United Kingdom has 10 major airports but it also has a larger number of small, regional airports, such as Norwich Airport and Bristol Airport. These link up to the international airports so that travellers can take domestic flights to the international airports and then fly on to their overseas destination. The 10 bigger airports are known as international airports because most of the holidaymakers travelling from them are travelling to other countries. The table below shows you the 10 international airports in the United Kingdom.

Airport	Location	Website
Belfast International	Belfast International Airport is situated just 18 miles north-west of Belfast and is accessed via a network of main roads and motorways. Take the M2 northbound, turn off at junction 5 and take the A57 for 7 miles.	www.belfastairport.com
Birmingham	Birmingham International Airport is on the A45 (Birmingham–Coventry) trunk road off junction 6 of the M42. There are direct connections to the M1, M5, M6 and M40.	www.bhx.co.uk
Cardiff	The airport is situated in Rhoose, 12 miles west of Cardiff city centre and 10 miles from junction 33 on the M4.	www.cardiffairportonline.com
East Midlands	East Midlands Airport is in the centre of the country, surrounded by the cities of Nottingham, Derby and Leicester and within easy reach of Sheffield, Stoke on Trent and Tamworth. Take the M1 northbound, continue along the M1 and come off at junction 23A then follow road signs to the airport.	www.eastmidlandsairport.com
Leeds/Bradford	The airport is signposted on all major roads over a wide area, including the M1 and M62 motorways and the Yorkshire section of the A1.	www.lbia.co.uk
London Gatwick	London Gatwick is 45kms (28 miles) south of London, directly linked to the M23 motorway at junction 9 and to the A23 London–Brighton road.	www.baa.co.uk/main/airports/gatwick
London Heathrow	Terminals 1, 2 & 3 are located in the centre of Heathrow and can be reached via the following motorways: M4 junction 4; M25 junction 15; A4 (local road). Terminal 4 is on the south side of Heathrow and can be reached via the following motorways: M4 junction 3; M25 junction 14; A30 (local road).	www.baa.co.uk/main/airports/heathrow
London Luton	London Luton Airport is only 30 minutes from North London, 15 minutes from the M25 and 5 minutes from the M1.	www.london-luton.co.uk
London Stansted	Situated next to junction 8a of the M11 motorway.	www.baa.co.uk/main/airports/stansted
Manchester	Manchester Airport is on the M56 motorway. It has a dedicated link road from the motorway at junction 5.	www.manairport.co.uk

Mark each of the 10 United Kingdom international airports on the map of the United Kingdom. Now mark your nearest local or regional airport. Find out if you can fly to one of the international airports from your local or regional airport.

FIND IT OUT

Eurotunnel

Rail

Trains provide a fast and largely reliable service. They avoid the problems of parking and can take travellers right into the centre of a town or city. The Eurotunnel and Eurostar link France and England, and the service runs every 15 minutes at peak times.

Train travel has many advantages over road travel, particularly by car:

- cars can be left at the station (although you have to pay to park);
- taxis are always available from stations;
- it is not so tiring to travel by train as it is to drive a car on a long journey;
- business people can work using laptops on a train;
- you can make telephone calls from a mobile telephone on a train, although they are banned from 'quiet' carriages;

- you can book your seats in advance;
- you can get cheaper travel by booking your ticket in advance;
- refreshments are available on trains (these are brought through the train on a trolley);
- buffet cars (serving hot food and drinks) are available on most trains.

Sea

The major ferry companies sail from the main ports in the United Kingdom (as shown in the table overleaf). Ferries are available for travel to the Isle of Wight, Northern Ireland, the Republic of Ireland, the Hebrides and the Shetland Islands. They provide a link to these destinations for both tourists and people travelling for business. Hovercraft and hydrofoils offer a faster ride across the water. The main routes are to Belgium, France and the Isle of Wight.

Sea cruises can also be taken down the Nile in Egypt or around the Mediterranean or Caribbean. They stop off at many exotic ports and are extremely popular, particularly with the older age group of traveller.

Major ferry ports in the United Kingdom

The major ferry ports in the United Kingdom are shown in the table on page 80. Find them on the map and draw a line to each of the destinations from those ports on the map. For instance, find Dover first and draw a line to Calais.

FIND IT OUT

Ferry port	Location	Website	Connects to
Dover	Port of Dover, Dover, Kent	www.doverport.co.uk	Up to 60 daily crossings to Calais, France. Up to five daily crossing to Zeebrugge, Belgium. Up to 3 daily crossings to Ostend, Belgium. Up to 10 daily crossings to Dunkerque, France.
Portsmouth	Continental Ferry Port, George Byng Way, Portsmouth, Hampshire PO2 8SP	www.portsmouth-port.co.uk	Multiple daily crossings to Cherbourg, Le Havre, Caen and St Malo, France. Two crossings per week to Bilbao, Spain. Daily crossings to St Helier, Jersey and St Peter Port, Guernsey. Multiple daily crossings to Fishbourne and Hyde, Isle of Wight.
Poole	Harbour Office, 20 New Quay Road, Hamworthy, Poole, Dorset BH15 4AF	www.phc.co.uk/10.htm	Up to two daily crossings to Cherbourg, France. Daily crossings to St Malo, France. Twice daily crossings to St Peter Port, Guernsey and St Helier, Jersey.
Holyhead	Port of Holyhead, Salt Island, Gwynedd, North Wales LL65 1DR	no website	Up to four daily crossings to Dun Laoghaire, Ireland. Twice daily crossings to the Port of Dublin and six daily crossings to the city of Dublin.
Harwich	Harwich International Port, Harwich, Essex	www.hph.com.hk/business/ports/europe/harwich.htm	Twice daily crossings to Hook of Holland. Three to four times weekly crossings to Cuxhaven, Germany. Three to four times weekly crossings to Eesbjerg, Denmark. Three times weekly crossings to Gothenburg, Sweden. Three times weekly crossings to Hamburg, Germany.
Larne	Larne Harbour Ltd, 9 Olderfleet Road, Larne, Co Antrim, Northern Ireland, BT40 1AS	www.portoflarne.co.uk	Larne–Cairnryan six to eight crossings daily. Larne–Troon. Larne–Fleetwood three crossings per day.

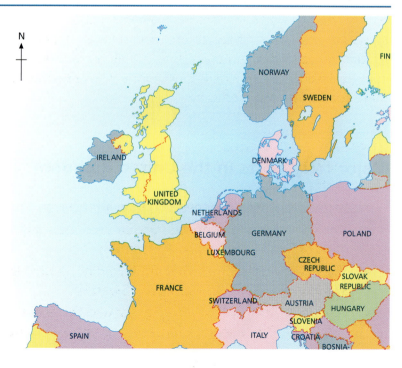

Road travel

Coach travel within the United Kingdom amounts to only 10% of customers travelling to their destinations. Coaches are a cheaper alternative to rail travel and have the following advantages:

- they can provide very flexible pick-up and drop-off points;
- they give the passenger good all-round views of the countryside and the scenery during the journey;
- most coaches now have toilets and videos;
- they are comparatively safe as drivers have a specific speed limit and number of hours they can drive.

Travelling on the road by car is not always reliable or relaxing. Although it is convenient because the driver can stop whenever he or she wants to, sometimes the amount of traffic can mean that you are not even able to get out of the car for a long time.

Long delays on the road can cause chaos if you are travelling to an airport in order to check in for a flight. The same applies if you are a businessman or woman who is driving to a meeting.

Major motorways in the United Kingdom

As cars, lorries and other vehicles grew in number in the United Kingdom, there was a need to improve the road network. Around 50 years ago motorways were built up and down the country, linking the major cities and ports in an attempt to make road travel more efficient.

England and Wales
- The M1 motorway runs from London via Leicester and Sheffield to Leeds.
- The M2 motorway connects London with Dover.
- The M3 motorway connects London with the south coast ports of Southampton and Portsmouth.
- The M4 motorway runs west from London, past Reading, Swindon and Bath, to Cardiff and Swansea.
- The M5 motorway links Birmingham and Exeter via Worcester, Cheltenham, Gloucester, Bristol and Taunton.

- The M6 motorway runs south from Carlisle to connect with the M1 beyond Coventry, making it simpler to reach Liverpool, Manchester, Stoke-on-Trent and Birmingham.
- The M20 motorway runs from the outskirts of London to Folkestone.
- The M25 motorway is an enormous ring road around London, with connections to the M1, M2, M3, M4, M11, M20, M23 and the M40.
- The M62 motorway connects Manchester with Liverpool.

Scotland

- A74 (M) from the Borders becoming the M74 to Glasgow.
- M80 from Glasgow to Stirling.
- M90 from Edinburgh to Kinross.
- M77 from Kilmarnock area to Glasgow.
- M8 from Glasgow to the Firth of Clyde.
- M9 from Stenhousemuir to Dunblane.

Northern Ireland

- The M1 motorway connects Belfast and Dungannon via Lisbern, Lurgan and Portadown.
- The M2 motorway connects Belfast with Ballymena via Antrim.

Using the map, draw in the motorways to connect the major cities by road. You could add some of the other major motorways we have not mentioned in a different colour.

Think
IT THROUGH

Main United Kingdom tourism destinations

There are a number of different types of tourism destinations throughout the country and they can be mainly broken up into the following categories:

- coastal areas, such as seaside towns and heritage coasts;
- countryside areas, such as national parks, areas of outstanding natural beauty, forests, mountain areas and lakes;
- tourist towns and cities;
- sporting venues;
- theme parks;
- places of historic interest.

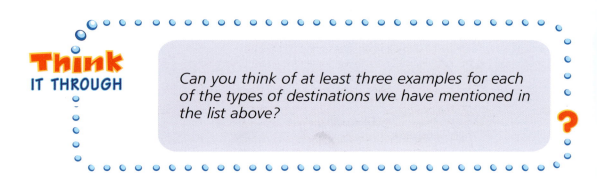

Think IT THROUGH

Can you think of at least three examples for each of the types of destinations we have mentioned in the list above?

Each type of destination is popular to visitors to the United Kingdom and to those who live here permanently, and this means that the tourism industry brings money into the country.

Coastal areas – seaside towns

The table on page 85 shows just how many important seaside towns there are in the United Kingdom. We are surrounded by water and this gives us the advantage of having many seaside resorts.

Tourism to these seaside resorts is popular, not only to those of us living in the United Kingdom, but also to visitors to our country.

Seaside towns	Major attractions	Website
Blackpool	Miles of beaches, Blackpool Tower, Sandcastle Complex, Tower Circus, Pleasure Beach, Blackpool shops, tenpin bowling, Blackpool Zoo, Stanley Park, golfing and bowls.	www.blackpooltourism.com/portal.asp
Bournemouth	Vistarama Balloon, Imax cinema, Bournemouth Oceanarium, Russell Cotes museum, The Pavilion, the Bournemouth International Centre.	www.bournemouth.co.uk
Brighton	Brighton Fishing Museum, Brighton Museum and Art Gallery, Childhood Museum, Palace Pier, Pavilion and Sea Life Centre.	www.visitbrighton.com
Llandudno	Llandudno is Wales's largest resort, situated between the Great Orme and Little Orme with two beaches, the award winning North Shore and the quiet, sand duned West Shore.	www.llandudno-tourism.co.uk
Portrush	Northern Ireland's favourite holiday destination. Attractions include the Royal Portrush golf course, long sandy beaches, night clubs, restaurants, Barry's, The Dunluce Centre, Waterworld and Fantasy Island. The surrounding area has the world famous Giant's Causeway, Dunluce Castle and Old Bushmills Distillery.	www.holidayportrush.com
Scarborough	Probably the world's first seaside resort, Scarborough has attracted visitors for almost 400 years. Scarborough is the 'queen of the Yorkshire Coast', with two bays, separated by the castle headland, the town is reached by Victorian cliff lifts. It has some of the finest formal gardens in Britain, shopping centre, variety of nightlife and family entertainment.	www.yorkshirecoast.co.uk/scarb/index.htm
Tenby	Pembrokeshire's main holiday resort. Major attractions include: Great Wedlock Dinosaur Park, Heatherton Country Sports Park, Grove Land Adventure World, Oakwood Theme Park and Kaleidoscope Discovery Centre.	www.visitpembrokeshire.co.uk
Torquay	Torquay's origins as a holiday resort date back to Victorian times when it was a fashionable destination for the English aristocracy. Torquay's waterfront is the focus of life in the town. Here you'll find the palm-lined promenade, seafront gardens, a lively harbour and an international marina.	www.theenglishriviera.co.uk

Coastal areas – heritage coasts

Heritage coast is a national designation to cover the most unspoilt areas of undeveloped coastline around England and Wales. It aims to identify and protect these unspoilt areas and make sure that housing developments, industry, pollution and tourism do not destroy them and that they are preserved as well as possible for future generations.

Countryside areas

As well as the national parks and the areas of outstanding natural beauty discussed below, there are also some countryside areas that appeal to tourists. These are:

- forests, such as the Thetford Forest in Norfolk;
- lakes, such as Lake Bala in Wales;
- mountains.

National parks in England and Wales

As you can see from the map on page 87, the United Kingdom's national parks are scattered around the country and many are situated in some of the most remote parts of England, Wales and Scotland. Many national parks are well known for their heather, moorlands, or their dramatic coastlines and mountainous areas.

The 11 national parks in England and Wales were established under the National Parks and Access to the Countryside Act of 1949. The New Forest, South Downs and the Cairngorms will soon join them.

FIND IT OUT

Visit the Association of National Parks Authorities website at www.anpa.gov.uk and find out the answers to the following questions:

1. How many square miles is the Brecon Beacons National Park?

2. *How many people live and work on Dartmoor?*

3. *How many people visit the Lake District each year?*

4. *In which park is Hadrian's Wall?*

5. *Which of the parks is the largest and how many square miles does it cover?*

National parks in England and Wales

Areas of outstanding natural beauty (AONB)

Areas of outstanding natural beauty (AONB) are not new. The concept was developed in the 1949 National Parks and Access to the Countryside Act. This was in recognition of the fact that there were areas of England and Wales that, although equally beautiful, could not share the national parks' recreational brief. These were called AONBs. Today there are 41 in England and Wales, representing some of the best farmed lowland and upland landscapes.

Their primary purpose is the conservation and enhancement of natural beauty, landscape, natural and historic heritage. However, there is a recognition that this natural beauty relies upon the management of the landscape through agriculture and forestry, and the economic and social activities that take place within it.

Tourist towns in the United Kingdom

As well as the seaside towns and resorts that we have already discussed there are a number of towns and cities that also appeal to visitors, both from the United Kingdom and from other countries. Many of these places have a long history and have attractions that can keep tourists busy for days. The table on page 90 shows you some of the most important tourist towns in the country.

FIND IT OUT

Visit one of the tourist town or city websites and create a two-day long schedule for a visitor to that town or city. Make sure that they see all of the most important sites or attractions possible and guess how long it would take to see each one. You may not be able to fit very many of the sites in with just two days to see them all!

Many of the other major tourist destinations in the United Kingdom are places we have already discussed in some detail. These are:

- *Sporting venues* – including all the premiership stadiums, national stadiums and stadiums related to hockey, rugby, cricket and golf.
- *Theme parks* – all of the major attractions, including Alton Towers, Legoland, Thorpe Park and Chessington World of Adventure.

case study

The Isle of Wight

About half of the Isle of Wight is an AONB, mostly in the south and west, but with five parcels stretching across the whole land area, in total around 189 square kilometres. It was designated in 1963. The AONB represents the variety of landscapes found upon the Island, from high chalk downs to lush green pastures. It also includes around half of the coastline including the entire heritage coast.

Centuries of land management have shaped the existing landform to create today's landscape. The combination of this variety with the maritime influence has produced the special feel of the AONB. The grand chalk cliffs and rolling downs, muddy creeks and estuaries, lush green pastures and trees and hedgerows share the same designation. It is this very variety that has given the island national importance.

Q1 *Name the six towns along the Tennyson heritage coast.*

Q2 *Name four towns not in an area of outstanding natural beauty.*

Q3 *What do you understand by the term 'land management'?*

- *Places of historic interest* – most can be found in the major tourist cities and towns. London, for example, has Buckingham Palace and the Tower of London and Edinburgh has its castle. Other places of historic interest are more remote, such as Stonehenge in the middle of the Wiltshire countryside.

Tourist towns	Major attractions	Website
Bath	Abbey, Assembly Rooms, Botanical Gardens, Costume Museum, Jane Austen Centre, Pump Rooms, Roman Baths, Royal Crescent and Theatre Royal.	www.visitbath.co.uk
Cambridge	Archaeology and Anthropology Museum, Botanic Gardens, Cambridge University, Christ's College and Sedgwick Museum.	www.cambridge.gov.uk/leisure/ TICWEB/tourism.htm
Chester	Tourist attractions in and around Chester include: Arley Hall, Catalyst – Science Discovery Centre, Tales of Historic Chester, Chester Cathedral, Cheshire Military Museum, Chester Zoo and On the Air – Broadcasting Museum.	www.chestercc.gov.uk/ visitingindex.html
Edinburgh	Edinburgh's main tourist attractions are: the Castle, Royal Mile, Palace of Holyrood, Holyrood Abbey, Holyrood Park, Arthur's Seat, Kirk of St Giles, Greyfriars, Edinburgh Zoo and the Royal Yacht Britannia.	www.edinburgh.org
London	London has many major tourist attractions. Some of the most famous are: British Airways London Eye, London Dungeon, British Museum, Madam Tussaud's, Tower of London, Buckingham Palace, Docklands, London Zoo, HMS Belfast and London Planetarium.	www.londontouristboard.com
Oxford	All Souls College, Ashmolean Museum, Balliol College, Bodleian Library, Botanic Gardens, Brasenose College, History of Science Museum, Museum of Modern Art, Museum of Oxford and University Museum.	www.oxfordcity.co.uk/guide/ infocent.html
Stratford-upon-Avon	Stratford-upon-Avon, otherwise known simply as Stratford, is the second most visited place in the United Kingdom, after London. Attractions include: Anne Hathaway's Cottage, (Mary) Arden's House, Museum of Shakespeare's Birthplace, Royal Shakespeare Company, Royal Shakespeare Theatre and World of Shakespeare.	www.stratford.co.uk
York	All Saints Church, Astrological Observatory, Automata Museum, City Art Gallery, Clifford's Tower, Jorvik Viking Centre, Minster, National Railway Museum and the Shambles.	www.touristnetuk.com/ne/York/ index.htm

Social, economic and environmental impact of tourism

The more attractive a travel location and the easier it is to get there, the more people will visit it. This might sound as if it is exactly what the businesses at the location want. More customers mean more profit, more jobs for the local population and generally good times for the area. The problem is that tourists bring many problems with them:

- Pollution (from their cars, the flights they take, from litter and from dealing with their waste).
- Crowds and queues (this might put off tourists from coming again and they will tell other people that the area was too busy).
- Damage to roads, footpaths, scenery, plants, animal life and buildings (more people means more wear and tear).
- The local population will find it difficult to get on with their own daily business as the area is swarming with tourists, the roads will be busy and the shops will be packed.
- Noise pollution will be a problem with visitors' cars, coaches and other transport.

Success and popularity are problems in themselves. The area might be very busy for three or four months of the year and empty for the rest of the year. If the area is very popular there will be a demand for houses that can be converted into guesthouses and hotels. This means that there will be fewer houses available for the locals. If the visitors like the area enough, they might even be tempted to buy a house there. More people hunting for houses lead to higher prices, which could mean that locals cannot afford to buy.

If buildings are converted into tourist businesses, like hotels, restaurants, shops and other facilities, when the tourists are not there they are likely to be closed with much less for the local people to do and to see themselves. An area can simply become too popular, ruining the place for tourists and locals alike. Moreover, if it continues to be popular and attracts more visitors, the very reasons that people want to come may be destroyed.

As part of your course you will need to look at two different tourist destinations and how they have, or have not, managed to cope with increasing levels of tourism. The Lake District and Stonehenge are two good examples of attempts to deal with the way tourism can affect either areas of outstanding natural beauty or historic sites.

Employment opportunities in the travel and tourism industry

Travel consultants

A travel consultant is the industry's name for someone who helps customers decide which holiday package or travel arrangements would best suit them. You can be a travel consultant in a travel agency or in the offices of a tour operator. You could also help rail travellers over the telephone or work for a coach travel firm.

Conference organisers

A conference organiser's job is to arrange everything that may be needed for a business or a group of people to meet together to either discuss or show one another their products and services. Conference organisers can have very busy lives as there is a great deal to be arranged if the conference is a large one and accommodation, food and refreshments, and entertainment needs to be part of the whole package.

Coach drivers

Coach drivers need to have a public service vehicle (PSV) licence to prove that they are trained and safe to drive buses and coaches and ensure that passengers are safe.

In the United Kingdom alone there are 55 000 local bus services, and over 4000 new ones are registered each year.

The Lake District is an ideal example of the problems of being too popular. The Lake District is a national park and one of the most visited areas of the United Kingdom. It has beautiful mountains and lakes and offers a large range of activities such a boating, walking, climbing and historic interest.

As the years have passed, its popularity and the activities have caused problems:

- popular walking areas suffer from erosion;
- mountain bikes and horses spoil the landscape by churning up the grass into mud;
- speedboats create noise pollution which annoys other boat users and tourists;
- cars cause traffic jams at popular times and air pollution;
- there are not enough parking spaces for cars so they have to park in the road and on grass;
- tourists park in front of farmers' gates;
- tourists drop litter and pick wild flowers.

Steps have been taken to try to deal with the situation and others are being planned:

- some roads are completely closed and others can be closed except for local traffic;
- a park-and-ride scheme could be created;
- speed restrictions on lakes;
- limit public access to footpaths and fenced-off areas.

Q1 *What do you understand by the word 'erosion'?*

Q2 *Why might a business on a busy road be more happy with the suggestions than a business on a road that is closed to traffic?*

Q3 *Suggest another two ways in which the Lake District could be saved from being too popular with the tourists.*

case study

Stonehenge

Stonehenge is in Wiltshire and is as old as the Egyptian pyramids. Stonehenge is protected and run by English Heritage. The site attracts thousands of visitors each year. In the past, visitors were able to walk through the stones and touch them, but now they are fenced off.

The site itself has had large amounts of money spent on it over the past few years. The car park is larger, and there is a gift shop, a restaurant and toilets. There are plans to develop the site even further with a large multimedia centre and other facilities.

The site is also a holy place for druids (a religious group) who come to worship there on the longest day of the year. English Heritage does not allow the druids to walk amongst the stones or to have large numbers of people present on that day.

Despite all of the development, the stones suffer from pollution from the nearby road and the fact that the site is open to the weather. This is causing concern as the stones cannot be replaced. There are plans to build a tunnel to hide the road and return the landscape to what it may have looked like when the stones were brought to the site thousands of years ago. Moving the road may help to protect the stones for future generations of visitors.

Currently, more than 800 000 people a year go through the turnstiles to see Stonehenge and at least another 200 000 stand at the roadside and peer through the fence. In August 2002, English Heritage chairman Sir Neil Cossons announced a £57 million visitor centre to replace the poor facilities used by almost a million people a year.

Funding will be £11.7 million from English Heritage, at least £10 million confirmed by the government and £26 million promised by the Heritage Lottery Fund.

Q1 *What type of attraction is Stonehenge?*

Q2 *What might happen to the visitor numbers if the Stonehenge site is developed further?*

Q3 *Where might the rest of the money needed for the development of the site come from?*

At the moment there are 8000 PSV licence holders in England and Wales, so coach driving is a popular occupation.

Not all coach drivers operate just in the United Kingdom. Many are expected to take passengers into Europe, via a ferry or through the Channel Tunnel. They will need to know what the rules of the road are in other countries. Normally, on long-haul journeys, there will be two coach drivers on each coach so that they can rest between shifts. Some coach drivers also act as guides, giving the passengers information about the different countries they may be travelling through, or pointing out areas of particular interest. They often do this via a hands-free microphone. Other coach companies employ a courier to travel with the driver to do this commentary for the passengers and to be on hand to answer any questions the passengers may have.

Air cabin crew

A flight attendant is responsible for the well-being and safety of passengers. In addition to serving food, drinks and **duty free** goods they also need to be a mine of information. They have to be prepared to deal with just about anything, including caring for unaccompanied children and administering first aid.

This job would give you the chance to meet many different people and, although you will probably start on domestic services (flights within the United Kingdom), you can work up to longer flights with the opportunity to visit more exotic locations.

The minimum age for flight attendants is usually 20 years old and some airlines will take on staff up to the age of 50. To do this job you would need to be able to:

- work well in a team;
- have a good standard of general education;
- be able to speak clear, concise English;
- be of smart appearance;
- be able to swim;
- be flexible – airlines work around the clock so early starts and late finishes can be expected. Service disruption can sometimes lead to delays and flight attendants must learn to accept these and keep smiling! A degree of stamina is needed as flying long distances can cause tiredness and jet lag.

On longer distance or long-haul flights, there may be overnight stays, or even stops of several days, so you will have the chance to see new places.

THE JARGON DRAGON

duty free – items such as alcohol, cigarettes and perfume that can be purchased on international flights at a lower price, as they do not include tax.

Tourist guide

The Blue Badge is the qualification of the United Kingdom's professional, registered tourist guides. The first Blue Badges were awarded to tourist guides who were trained for the Festival of Britain in 1951. There are now around 2000 Blue Badge guides in England and Wales, just over half of whom are London-based. To be a Blue Badge guide you must:

- enjoy working with people;
- be physically fit and have a lot of stamina;
- understand the stresses and strains encountered by travellers;

- always offer a warm welcome;
- be able to deal with problems in an efficient and professional way and be able to keep smiling!

Resort representative

The job of a resort representative would give you the chance to meet a lot of people and visit interesting locations, either in the United Kingdom or around the world. Generally you will find yourself working in a team, spending most of the day outdoors. Every day is different so this job is not suitable for someone who likes a 9-to-5 routine. Many of the tasks listed will be common to each job, wherever you are located:

- Responsibility for the well-being and safety of customers. You will meet them at the airport, port or railway station and transfer them to their accommodation, making sure that they are comfortable and that all their needs are met.
- Provide customers with information, especially about local attractions. You may arrange excursions and often accompany them, as well as contacting local transport companies, hotels and restaurants.
- You should be prepared to deal with just about anything, including caring for children, administering first aid and sorting out any problems that may occur. Some companies like to provide welcome parties so the representative will make the arrangements and host the event, telling clients about the resort facilities and local area, and promoting attractions.
- You will stay on or near the holiday location and, if responsible for a wide area, will be provided with means of transportation (either a small car or a moped). For camping holidays, representatives will normally be accommodated on site in a tent.
- The age limit will depend on the type of representative you want to be. The lower age limit is usually 18 years but some companies, especially those catering for customers in higher age groups, recruit staff up to the age of 70. To take a position as an overseas representative you will need to be at least 21 years old.

If you wanted to become a resort representative you would need to be able to:

- work well in a team;
- have a good standard of general education;
- be of smart appearance;
- be able to speak good, clear English – being able to communicate with people of all ages and backgrounds will be a considerable advantage, as will the ability to speak one or more additional European languages;
- be very flexible, as a tour representative will be on duty around the clock;
- be able to use a word processor for the paperwork and reports;
- be available to give advice and to resolve problems at virtually any time of the day;
- show a pleasant, outgoing personality;
- be a good organiser and a practical person with plenty of common sense.

You could work virtually in any holiday location worldwide, although the majority of resorts will probably be found within Europe. Locations will include beach, lake, mountain and city holiday centres and many of these are year-round destinations. For those who would prefer not to be based abroad there are opportunities to work as a resort representative in the United Kingdom.

FIND IT OUT

As we have already mentioned, there are hundreds of different types of jobs in the travel and tourism industry. Visit the two websites you went to before – www.jobsearch.co.uk and www.monster.co.uk – and search for jobs, which you will find under 'travel' or 'tourism'. Can you find any jobs in the industry for which you could apply?

Bringing leisure and tourism together

As you have now seen, it is often very difficult to separate leisure and tourism because often they rely on one another so much. A leisure visit to a local cinema may mean that you will visit a takeaway afterwards and will need to use public transport to get there and back. Even the bigger attractions, such as theme parks, need transport and catering, either organised by themselves, or by other businesses.

When you go to a different part of the country to visit an attraction you are a tourist, so that makes your leisure time a tourist activity. If you visited a city to go to the theatre or visit a museum and needed to stay overnight, you would be using both the leisure and the tourism industries.

It is often the case that leisure facilities such as cinemas, libraries and sports centres have details about local transport and at railway stations or bus garages you will find leaflets about attractions that you can visit in the area. They all rely on one another, which is why it is sometimes difficult to know what is leisure and what is tourism.

Marketing

What's in this unit?

This unit discusses the importance of marketing in today's leisure and tourism industries. All leisure and tourism organisations, regardless of the products or services they provide, use the same basic marketing ideas. These help them to ensure that they sell the right product to the right people in the right place at the right price using the right promotion. Both of the industries are very competitive and customers demand a great deal from them.

Most people tend to think that marketing is just advertising but it is much wider and more important to a business than that. Organisations need to decide what to sell, to whom they will sell it and the best way to tell those people what they want to sell. They also need to worry about what other businesses are doing and what prices to charge for their products and services. All of this is marketing.

You will also learn about the four main marketing tools used by organisations:

- target marketing;
- market research;
- the marketing mix;
- SWOT (strengths-weaknesses-opportunities-threats) analysis.

This unit is assessed internally through a portfolio of your work on the marketing activities of leisure and tourism organisations. You will also need to look in detail at one organisation and produce some promotional material for it.

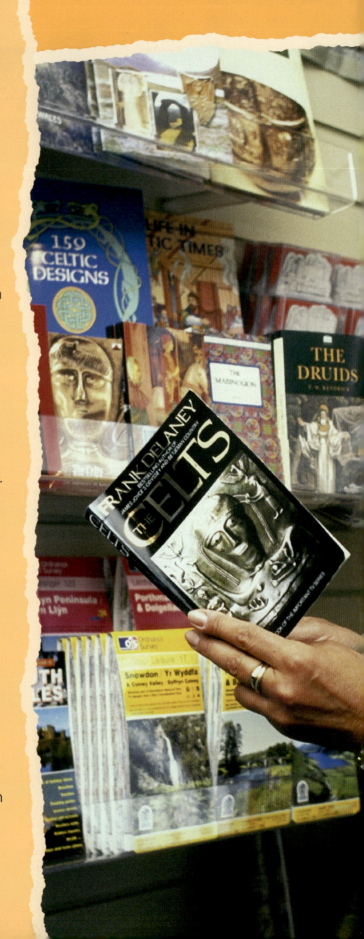

In this unit you will learn about:

The importance of marketing in leisure and tourism

THE JARGON DRAGON

competitive – many different businesses trying to attract the same group of customers

Like many other areas of business, the leisure and tourism industry is very **competitive**. There are always a limited number of customers, whether they are people interested in visiting a tourist attraction, using a leisure centre or buying a holiday package. Each of the organisations in the industry must try to convince people that they should spend their time and their money with it and not someone else or somewhere else.

Most towns, cities and areas of the United Kingdom have their own tourist boards. This is often where the marketing begins, with the local council helping to support the marketing efforts of the organisations and businesses in the area to achieve success. Each organisation or business in the leisure and tourism industry will attempt to attract as many customers as possible and, as we will see, they use a variety of different methods to do this.

FIND IT OUT

What does your local council do to help support the marketing efforts of leisure and tourism businesses in the area? You should be able to find out from the council itself, a tourist information centre or your local library. Does the council have particular plans and schemes? Collect some leaflets showing leisure activities going on in your region.

What is marketing?

There are many definitions of **marketing**. They all mention the fact that marketing is concerned with making sure that the customer is satisfied, but the role of marketing is deeper than that. Before a business can satisfy a customer's needs, it needs to know who its customers are and what they want. It is also important for the business to make sure that everyone working for it and who has contact with customers is aiming to give the customer the best time and experience possible. Marketing should also include taking account of what customers might say, and doing something about it. Finally, marketing should also help the business think ahead into the future and work out what customers might want and how things could be improved.

To sum up, what exactly is marketing and what does it do for the business?

- Marketing focuses on the satisfaction of customer **needs**, **wants** and requirements.
- Everyone who has contact with customers needs to think about satisfying customers and this should be the most important thought.
- Future customer needs have to be identified and anticipated.
- Alongside thinking about customer satisfaction and customer needs, the business may need to think about its **profits**. After all, if the business spends too much on making sure that the customers are happy then there won't be a great deal of money left.

On the question of marketing and money, it would be easy to spend too much on marketing. Everything that a leisure and tourism organisation produces to market its products and services costs money. Colour brochures are expensive and television advertising costs even more – few leisure and tourism businesses can afford such things. They have to come up with other ways of marketing that are cheaper but equally effective.

As we will see, marketing is all about getting the balance right, doing what needs to be done within the **budget** that the

THE JARGON DRAGON

marketing – getting the right product to the right people in the right place at the right price using the right promotion

needs – essential products and services required by customers (food, housing and transport)

wants – products or services desired by customers (entertainment and luxuries, which include holidays)

profits – what is left from a business's income after costs have been paid

THE JARGON DRAGON

budget – the amount of money available to a leisure and tourism organisation to spend on marketing

marketing mix – also known as the 'four Ps': product, place, price and promotion, all the ingredients needed to get the marketing right

business has. The keys to this are called the **marketing mix**, or the 'four Ps'. These are:

- product – what the business offers; it can be a service such as a swimming lesson or a product such as a souvenir;
- place – where the product is available, the location of the tourist attraction or where the customer can buy the service, such as a holiday package from a travel agent;
- price – does the product offer the customer good value for money and how does the price compare to the prices offered by the competitors;
- promotion – how does the business tell the customers what products are available and where they are available.

We will return to the marketing mix later and look at the 'four Ps' in more detail.

Think IT THROUGH

Do you think your school might have a marketing budget? If it had one, what do you think it would be trying to promote?

FIND IT OUT

Have a look through some newspaper articles. Can you find any that tell you about a particular company that has spent a lot of money on a new advertisement? If so, what is the business promoting? What is the purpose of the advertisement?

Target marketing

It is not possible to tell everyone about your leisure facility or tourist attraction – unless you are a massive organisation such as Disney or Madame Tussauds, who can afford the national coverage. So, you need to target those that might be interested. In any case, not everyone is going to want to use your facilities. Senior citizens, for example, might not be interested in extreme sports such as snowboarding or white-water rafting and younger people might not be interested in visiting a tourist town that does not have takeaways or night clubs.

This is why organisations tend to target the groups of people that are more likely to be interested. There is little to be gained by telling people who are not interested and who won't come anyway no matter what you promise them.

Whenever you think about any part of the leisure and tourism industry consider at whom it is aimed. Theme parks might be aimed at families, sleepy traditional seaside towns at older people, and night clubs at the younger age groups. Some facilities, attractions and services are aimed at everyone but few succeed in managing to attract them all.

Take a visit to a local travel agent and have a look at the range of holiday brochures. Find at least three different brochures that are aimed at particular types of customer. The covers might give you a clue about who they are aimed at. Try to find three that are aimed at very different groups of people, either by age, family size or interests. Ask whether you can take them with you and look at what they are offering. Make a list of the main features that might appeal to the target group that the brochure is aimed at.

A large business that offers holiday packages might actually target several different groups of people and have a variety of different types of products and services, but they are all offered by the same business. It helps customers to identify quickly something that might be of interest to them.

Market segmentation

THE JARGON DRAGON

market segmentation – splitting up all customers into groups which have similar characteristics (such as age or gender)

buying habits – how particular customers purchase things; whether they buy them in a shop, on the Internet or by mail order and how often they buy (does the customer use the leisure facility each week or how many holidays does the customer take each year?)

segment – a group of customers that have similar characteristics and buying habits

Market segmentation involves identifying different groups of customers within a market. Each person in a group will have similar characteristics; they have similar needs and similar **buying habits**. The world is made up of billions of buyers with their own sets of needs and behaviour. What segmentation tries to do is identify these groups of customers and each group is known as a **segment**.

It is not always easy to carry out segmentation. Each of the segments needs to be able to provide the following information to the business; otherwise the segment is not worth trying to provide products and services for:

- Is the segment big enough? In other words, are there enough customers who want to buy the products and can the business make a profit from it?
- Is the segment easy to reach? In other words, how easy is it for the business to enter the segment with its marketing?

Thomson Holidays

case study

Thomson Holidays, a division of TUI UK Ltd, is the largest tourism and services group in the world, employing 80 000 people in 500 companies around the globe. Thomson Holidays' head office is in London but the majority of its 3000 employees work overseas. The company has about one-third of the United Kingdom market and operates to a wide range of resorts offering a variety of holiday types to suit all ages and tastes.

In addition to the widest choice of hotels and apartments in a variety of destinations, it also offers a range of different types of holidays suited to different types of people. Here are some examples:

Thomson Gold is designed with couples in mind – from approved menus to tables for two. They don't accept bookings for children under 16.

Young at Heart holidays are designed for the over-55s only and include both relaxing and activity holidays.

Weddings in Paradise are aimed at couples wanting to get married in exotic locations around the world. The service is basically a marriage ceremony and honeymoon in one package.

(Source: adapted from www.thomson.co.uk)

Q1 *Visit www.thomson.co.uk, which is Thomson's website, and find out what different types of holidays it offers. To how many different groups of people does it offer holidays? How do the holidays they offer to different people differ?*

Q2 *Why do most of the employees work overseas? What do they do?*

Q3 *Design your own type of holiday package that does not cater for a group already provided for by Thomson. Make it a holiday for one week. What will you call it? Who is it aimed at and what are the main features of the package? You could even design your own logo and produce a leaflet to advertise it. You could use this in later activities when you have to produce promotional material.*

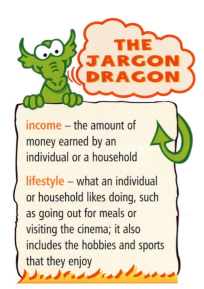

income – the amount of money earned by an individual or a household

lifestyle – what an individual or household likes doing, such as going out for meals or visiting the cinema; it also includes the hobbies and sports that they enjoy

- Is the segment measurable? Can the business obtain information to consider whether it is worth pursuing?

If the segment does not measure up to these criteria, then it is probably not worth the expense of researching the segment any further. Segmentation is not just about making segments by customers' ages or even their **income** – segments can be made up from many different measurements, such as where people live, whether they have children or their **lifestyle**.

We will look at these ways to measure and organise a segment in a little more detail and discuss how some of them may be useful in recognising the characteristics of customers.

Age

Age is a useful of way of segmenting the market but on its own it may not be enough to segment the market accurately. Age does not really tell us very much about what people like, buy or their habits. Typically, the market can be segmented in terms of age bands such as:

Under 16
17–21
22–26
27–31
32–39
40–45
46–50
51–60
60+

The only problem with using age as a way of segmenting the market is whether you can assume that all those between 17 and 21 are similar. Obviously, people are very different even though they are the same age. What you can guess from age is the fact that the older you are the more likely you are to have money, as you will probably be working. This still doesn't help, though, because even those who are over 60 and may have retired still don't like the same things and don't behave the same way either.

Think
IT THROUGH

Do all the people in your class like to do the same things? Discuss this as a group and you will probably discover that even though you are in the same age group, what appeals to one of you might not appeal to others.

FIND IT OUT

A simple way to prove that age is not a good enough method of segmenting the market is to carry out a straightforward piece of research. Write down the top five things you enjoy doing in your leisure time and then ask 10 people in your class (who are the same age) what their top five are too. How many of your top five are the same as the others?

Now write a list of things people in older age groups do. What else does the older age group do that you don't do?

Gender

We all know that there are differences between males and females, but can we assume that they are so very different in what they like? Just how useful would it be to segment the market in terms of gender?

Actually it is quite useful because not only do men and women like to do different things – they also react to different types of marketing too.

case study

Marketing health clubs to women

Statistics show that 32.8 million Americans are paying to be members of health clubs. Of these members, 51.6% are women. Today, in all sectors, women are more important consumers than ever. According to some researchers, women buy or influence the purchase of 80% of all consumer goods.

Research has also shown that marketing to women works when the following rules are followed:

- Women like a softer approach to selling than men, such as softer colours (when possible), more feminine fonts and tasteful photos that focus on groups and families.

- Women are much more likely to buy a product when it has been recommended to them. Women also like free trial periods, money-back guarantees and short-term programmes that allow them to try out a leisure facility at little or no risk.

- Women hate to be sold something – they like to buy. In fact, even deeper than that, women love the process of buying. This is why a woman can go out for an entire day of shopping, come home with nothing but have had a fabulous time.

- By discovering and understanding what women like in advertising, sales and member services, clubs will position themselves to take full advantage of the growing women's market.
(Source: adapted from *Club Industry* February 2002.)

Q1 *If the total number of Americans using health clubs is 32.8 million and the percentage of women is 51.6%, what is the actual number of American women using health clubs in America?*

Q2 *What do you understand by the term 'consumer goods'?*

Q3 *Design your own poster for a health club to attract female customers, taking account of the advice in the case study.*

Social group

Social group is another way of describing the class to which people belong. This form of segmentation uses occupation and income as a way to categorise people. The National Statistics Socio-economic Classifications (NS-SEC) is the latest way of describing the different social classes in the United Kingdom. These used to be grouped as A, B, C and so forth, so if you do any research on older material, that is how the socio-economic groups would have been classified. The current classification system is as follows:

1. Higher managerial and professional occupations
    1.1   Employers and managers in larger organisations (for example, company directors, senior company managers, senior civil servants, senior officers in police and armed forces)
    1.2   Higher professionals (for example, doctors, lawyers, clergy, teachers, social workers)
2. Lower managerial and professional occupations (for example, nurses and midwives, journalists, actors, musicians, prison officers, lower ranks of police and armed forces)
3. Intermediate occupations (for example, clerks, secretaries, driving instructors, telephone fitters)
4. Small employers and own account workers (for example, publicans, farmers, taxi drivers, window cleaners, painters and decorators)
5. Lower supervisory, craft and related occupations (for example, printers, plumbers, television engineers, train drivers, butchers)
6. Semi-routine occupations (for example, shop assistants, hairdressers, bus drivers, cooks)
7. Routine occupations (for example, couriers, labourers, waiters, refuse collectors)
8. Plus an eighth category to cover those who have never had paid work and the long term unemployed.

Social class has not always been measured like this. The new way of describing the social classes in the United Kingdom has replaced the older version, which was:

I Professional occupations
II Managerial and technical occupations
IIIN Skilled non-manual occupations
IIIM Skilled manual occupations
IV Partly skilled occupations
V Unskilled occupations
VI Armed forces

Think
IT THROUGH

Using the information that you gathered for the last activity, place each of the parents or guardians in these six categories. Was it easy to place them or harder?

?

Advertisers and market researchers use a similar way of working out social classes, known as the 'ABC1' scale:

GROUP A
Professional workers (lawyers, doctors and so forth), scientists, managers of large-scale organisations.

GROUP B
Shopkeepers, farmers, teachers, white-collar workers.

GROUP C
1. Skilled manual (hand) workers – high grade, for example master builders, carpenters, shop assistants, nurses.
2. Skilled manual – low grade, for example electricians, plumbers.

GROUP D
Semi-skilled manual, for example, bus drivers, lorry drivers, fitters.

GROUP E
Unskilled manual, for example, general labourers, barmen, porters.

- *Using the National Statistics Socio-economic Classifications suggest at least one leisure or tourism activity that each of the different classes might enjoy.*
- *South England Airlines has three types of seat on its aircraft: first class, business class and economy class. Each class has a different level of service and the price is also different. Give one example, for each 'class', of whom they hope to sell to, stating your reasons and giving the seating costs.*

Lifestyle

Lifestyle refers to the choice of hobbies, recreational pursuits, entertainment, holidays, and other non-worktime pursuits. Lifestyle is a person's way of life and can offer a great deal of information and be very useful in market segmentation.

People's lifestyles, everyday activities, interests, opinions and beliefs on certain issues have a lot to do with who they are. Marketing experts refer to them as AIOs (activities, interest and opinions) and our AIOs influence our everyday behaviour from where we shop to what we buy.

A business would wish to develop and aim products/services at particular lifestyle groups and develop lifestyle profiles on their target market. If we understand the lifestyle of a particular group we can sell it a product or service on the basis that it will enhance their lifestyle. A lifestyle group is a particular segment defined by the organisation that is marketing a product or service – for example single people, young couples or older couples with children. This lifestyle segment is labelled because individuals within it display similar characteristics.

case study

The VALS system

The American VALS system is one of the most commonly used ways to identify people by their lifestyle. It is useful in the sense that it looks both at the way people think and the resources (money) they have to do what they want. There are eight categories.

- Actualisers are successful, sophisticated, active, people who like to 'take charge'. They have high opinions of themselves and plenty of resources. They are interested in growth and seek to develop, explore and express themselves in a variety of ways.

- Fulfilleds are mature, satisfied, comfortable and thoughtful people who value order, knowledge and responsibility. Most are well educated and in professional occupations. They are well informed and happy with their careers, families and place in life. Their leisure activities tend to centre on the home.

- Achievers are successful career- and work-centred people who like to feel in control of their lives. They value calm and stability over risk. They are committed to work and family. Their social lives are structured around family, church and career.

- Experiencers are young, enthusiastic and rebellious. They seek variety and excitement and often the risky. They love new trends but soon get tired of them and move on to something new.

- Believers are traditional people with set ideas. They love routine and most of what they do centres on the home, social groups and organisations.

- Strivers want to feel secure as they have few resources of their own. For them, money is success but they can become very bored and may take risks.

- Makers are practical people and they have a traditional life of family, practical work, and physical recreation and have little interest in what lies outside these areas. Makers experience the world by doing practical things such as painting or gardening.

- Strugglers have difficult lives. They are poor, badly educated and low in skills. They want security and safety above all and their limited resources force them only to think of what they need at the moment.

Q1 *Do you recognise yourself as being one of these? Which category fits your best friend?*

Q2 *Think of at least one leisure and one tourism activity that might appeal to each of these eight categories. Give reasons for your choice.*

FIND IT OUT

Here is a brief description of what is known as the 'grey market'. The grey market is defined as being those people aged 50 years and over. Research based on information from Saga magazine readers shows that the grey market provides the United Kingdom with 40% of its total income, and owns between 70% and 80% of its wealth. Lifestyle groups within the grey market can be grouped as:

1. WOOPIES (well-off older persons) – these are married males living in two-person households. They are less than 75 years old, are well off, have an 86% investment income, and high home and car ownership.

2. OPALS (old people with affluent lifestyles).

3. JOLLIES (jet-setting oldies with lots of loot).

This is marketing language about lifestyles. Can you translate the information? Put it into your own words and try to think of an example of each of the three from the people you know.

Ethnicity

ethnic minorities – those of a different culture who make up part of the population of an area, region or country

People's needs and wants as customers may vary according to their religion, language, social customs, dietary habits and ethnic background. In the United Kingdom and abroad, leisure and tourism businesses have to provide for a wide range of different cultures, or **ethnic minorities**. For example, Muslims do not eat pork, and religious Jewish people celebrate their Sabbath on a Saturday.

Ethnicity is not only a useful way of segmenting the market for United Kingdom residents but it is also a good indication of the background of visitors from overseas:

Overseas tourism by country of residence (2001)

	Visits (Thousands)	Nights (Thousands)	Spending (£millions)
USA	3580	28 463	2383
France	2852	16 274	685
Germany	2309	14 182	731
Irish Republic	2039	8077	548
Netherlands	1411	5859	387
Belgium	916	2721	150
Italy	857	7186	417
Spain	856	8562	320
Australia	695	12 914	541
Canada	647	7395	318
Other countries	6673	77 883	4826
Total	22 835	189 516	11 306

Source: International Passenger Survey

FIND IT OUT

1. *What is the average number of nights spent in the United Kingdom by people from the United States, Belgium and Canada?*

2. *On average, which nationality spends the most per person in the United Kingdom on holidays?*

3. *The 'other countries' category is a large one. Suggest at least 10 nationalities that would be part of this figure.*

New customers and existing customers/ members and non-members

As we have seen in the previous unit, existing customers are very important to a business in the leisure and tourism industry. In fact, existing customers are so important that businesses are desperate to know what they think and what they need to do to keep them.

Why do you think that existing customers are so important to a business? Why does a business strive to find out what their customers think?

Remember that marketing is not just about attracting customers to the leisure or tourism product or service in the first place. It is very much about keeping customers when you have found them.

Customer loyalty has become a very important area of market research and is another way of segmenting the market, in other words judging exactly how loyal a customer is.

Type of existing customers	Characteristics	What should be done to keep them
Indifferent	Customer needs and wants that are basic to fulfilling the contract between you and them. For example, customers expect to be treated with courtesy and respect.	Make sure that customers are always considered and that their basic needs and wants are looked after. Giving them more than they expect will move them on to the next category.
Satisfied	This is where your customers actually tell you what is important to them. Meeting a customer's needs here will cause satisfaction.	It is vital to ensure that what customers ask for is given (within reason) in order to keep them satisfied. If the business does better than customers expect then they will be delighted.
Delighted	This is where a customer hopes for something and asks for it but really does not expect you to provide it. This is the business's opportunity to provide something beyond the customer's expectations and by doing this will create delight.	Not providing it will be unlikely to cause dissatisfaction, but this is the ideal opportunity to give customers what they want as this could convert them into *loyal* customers.
Loyal	Providing benefits above and beyond what customers are even aware of can create loyal customers. They will already be keen to use the business and will have hopes that they are treated as well as they have been in the past.	Keeping customers in this category requires the business to keep thinking about what other benefits they could offer them. Many customers will be prepared to pay for extras. Thinking about steadily improving what is on offer to the customer and then telling them about it is vital.

case study

The cost of losing customers

It has been estimated that it costs up to five times as much to win a new customer than it does to keep an existing one. One of the major reasons why customers will not buy from a business again is that they had a complaint to make and it was not dealt with in an efficient manner. Most customers will complain to front-line staff (those who deal with customers on a day-to-day basis) and only 1% to 5% have to take their complaint further. The most common complaint is that customers have been overcharged or charged for something they did not get (around 50% to 75% of all complaints). The second most common is mistreatment, poor quality and poor standards of service (between 5% and 30% of all complaints). Amazingly, only 3% of airline travellers who thought their in-flight meal was not up to standard made a complaint. All of these complained to the air cabin crew and did not take their complaint further.

Q1 *Who would be the front-line staff in a theme park?*

Q2 *If it cost a business £20 to obtain a new customer, how much would it cost to keep one?*

Q3 *List five other reasons why a customer may make a complaint on board an aircraft.*

New members of an organisation offer a different challenge in terms of segmentation, as apart from knowing the basics about them (such as name, address, age and telephone number) little is known about what they like and don't like. It is therefore harder to segment them.

Geographic

ACORN, the United Kingdom's original consumer classification, first developed in 1978, is used for segmenting the country's population in terms of consumer and lifestyle characteristics. It combines geography with **demographic** data from the **census** to classify the population into 17 groups, which are subdivided into 55 types. The census data include age, gender, marital status as well as occupation, education and home ownership.

THE JARGON DRAGON

ACORN – 'A Classification of Residential Neighbour-hoods', a segmentation method that uses the census to create 17 different groups and 55 different types of people

demographics – the study of population changes

census – a 10-yearly government questionnaire that requires every household in the United Kingdom to complete a form and answer basic questions about the number of people living there and type of house and so forth

Category	Group		Type
A Thriving	Wealthy achievers, suburban areas	1	Wealthy suburbs, large detached houses
		2	Villages with wealthy commuters
		3	Mature affluent home-owning areas
		4	Affluent suburbs, older families
		5	Mature, well-off suburbs
	Affluent greys, rural communities	6	Agricultural villages, home-based workers
		7	Holiday retreats, older people, home-based workers
	Prosperous pensioners, retirement areas	8	Home-owning areas, well-off older residents
		9	Private flats, elderly people
B Expanding	Affluent executives, family areas	10	Affluent working families with mortgages
		11	Affluent working couples with mortgages, new homes
		12	Transient workforce, living at its place of work

	Well-off workers, family areas	13	Home-owning family areas
		14	Home-owning family areas, older children
		15	Families with mortgages, younger children
C Rising	Affluent urbanites, town and city areas	16	Well-off town and city areas
		17	Flats and mortgages, singles and young working couples
		18	Furnished flats and bedsits, younger single people
	Prosperous professionals, metropolitan areas	19	Apartments, young professional singles and couples
		20	Gentrified multi-ethnic areas
	Better-off executives, inner city areas	21	Prosperous enclaves, highly qualified executives
		22	Academic centres, students and young professionals
		23	Affluent city centre areas, tenements and flats
		24	Partially gentrified multi-ethnic areas
		25	Converted flats and bedsits, single people
D Settling	Comfortable middle agers, mature home-owning areas	26	Mature established home-owning areas
		27	Rural areas, mixed occupations
		28	Established home-owning areas
		29	Home-owning areas, council tenants, retired people
	Skilled workers, home-owning areas	30	Established home-owning areas, skilled workers
		31	Home owners in older properties, younger workers
		32	Home-owning areas with skilled workers
E Aspiring	New home owners, mature communities	33	Council areas, some new home owners
		34	Mature home-owning areas, skilled workers
		35	Low-rise estates, older workers, new home owners
	White-collar workers, better-off multi-ethnic areas	36	Home-owning multi-ethnic areas, young families
		37	Multi-occupied town centres, mixed occupations
		38	Multi-ethnic areas, white-collar workers
F Striving	Older people, less prosperous areas	39	Home owners, small council flats, single pensioners
		40	Council areas, older people, health problems
	Council estate residents, better-off homes	41	Better-off council areas, new home owners
		42	Council areas, young families, some new home owners
		43	Council areas, young families, many lone parents

		44	Multi-occupied terraces, multi-ethnic areas
		45	Low-rise council housing, less well-off families
		46	Council areas, residents with health problems
	Council estate residents, high unemployment	47	Estates with high unemployment
		48	Council flats, elderly people, health problems
		49	Council flats, very high unemployment, singles
	Council estate residents, greatest hardship	50	Council areas, high unemployment, lone parents
		51	Council flats, greatest hardship, many lone parents
	People in multi-ethnic, low-income areas	52	Multi-ethnic, large families, overcrowding
		53	Multi-ethnic, severe unemployment, lone parents
		54	Multi-ethnic, high unemployment, overcrowding
	Unclassified	55	

Here is a version of the ACORN listing for the county of Hampshire.

Type of neighbourhood	Percentage nationally	Percentage in Hampshire
Wealthy achievers, suburban areas	14	27
Affluent greys, rural communities	2	1
Prosperous pensioners, retirement areas	3	6
Affluent executives, family areas	3	12
Well-off workers, family areas	7	9
Affluent urbanites, town and city areas	3	2
Prosperous professionals, metropolitan areas	3	0
Better-off executives, inner city areas	4	1
Comfortable middle agers, mature home-owning areas	14	15
Skilled workers, home-owning areas	11	7
New home owners, mature communities	10	7
White-collar workers, better-off multi-ethnic areas	4	1
Older people, less prosperous areas	4	3
Council estate residents, better-off homes	11	7
Council estate residents, high unemployment	4	1
Council estate residents, greatest hardship	2	1
People in multi-ethnic, low-income areas	2	0

Source: Adapted from information from Hampshire County Council

FIND IT OUT

Which of the categories in Hampshire is the most different from the national average? Would the area be a good place to set up a fitness centre for the grey market? Give reasons for your answer.

The 'wealthy achievers, suburban areas' is the largest ACORN group in Hampshire. Suggest three leisure facilities and three tourism facilities to suit their needs.

Businesses

First class airport lounge

Ecomony class airport lounge

Segmenting the market by identifying businesses as opposed to individual customers is also a very useful technique. Business customers look for different things from leisure and tourism compared to ordinary customers. Here are some facts about business travellers:

- 80% of businesses now operate a formal travel policy;
- 75% of these policies cover all four main aspects of business travel – air, hotels, car hire and rail travel;
- 75% of businesses feel that the service they receive from their travel management company, in terms of arranging business travel, is more important than five years ago;
- 75% of business travellers belong to a frequent-flyer scheme;

- around 50% of business travellers would be prepared to travel on less expensive no-frills flights on short-haul routes within Europe;
- 85% do not book travel electronically – currently, only 7% of businesses email their travel management company with business travel arrangements;
- most business travellers describe the experience of ticket-less travel as positive – quicker check-in procedures were mentioned by 40% of business travellers as the most relevant description of their experience with ticketless travel, and 26% described the system as problem free.

> *What do you think is meant by the terms 'formal travel policy' and 'ticketless travel'? Find out the name of one ticketless airline. Go to its website and see what benefits it brings. What does a travel management company do?*

FIND IT OUT

Business travel and tourism in the United Kingdom is worth millions of pounds to the leisure and tourism industry. The first of the two following tables shows the numbers of business tourism visits (in millions) between 1995 and 2001 (these are the latest figures available). The second table shows the amount of money (again in millions) spent by business tourists in the United Kingdom over the same period.

Business tourism visits (millions) 1995–2001

Year	United Kingdom	England	Scotland	Wales
1995	5.76	4.23	0.26	0.09
1996	6.10	4.32	0.26	0.10
1997	6.35	4.46	0.29	0.12
1998	6.88	4.89	0.30	0.10
1999	7.04	5.45	0.34	0.16
2000	7.32	5.72	0.27	0.17
2001	6.77	5.24	0.24	0.20

Source: International Passenger Survey (IPS)

Business tourism spending (£ millions) 1995–2001

Year	United Kingdom	England	Scotland	Wales
1995	3219	2716	127	29
1996	3220	2685	109	46
1997	3501	2968	140	37
1998	3820	3264	171	37
1999	3967	3595	194	63
2000	4048	3739	148	53
2001	3582	3284	125	61

Source: International Passenger Survey (IPS)

FIND IT OUT

Convert both tables into a graph using the United Kingdom figures with a second line for the part of the country you are in. Suggest reasons why England has the most business tourists and income from them.

Market research

Market research should be thought of as the organised collecting, analysing and presenting of useful marketing information. It should help a business identify, service and satisfy the needs and desires of its customers.

When a leisure and tourism business decides to do market research, it has a reason. Perhaps it needs questions answered about the way it is performing and the attitudes of customers. Market research should not be undertaken lightly as it can cost a great deal and it takes up the time of employees who will have to manage the research.

When not to do market research	When to do market research
When the business knows what it needs to know to make a decision	When the business needs information to make a decision
When useful information already exists	When the business is unsure of which available alternatives to choose
When there is little time before the decision needs to be made	When there are clear problems brought to the attention of the business by customers
When the cost of collecting the information is more than can be gained by what the market research reveals	When a business is thinking of launching a new product or service
When the business is unclear about what it wants to find out	When the business is certain it knows what it wants to research and how the research will help it make decisions

Many organisations (including the government) collect information that would be of use to a leisure or tourism business. If, for example, the business wanted to know about the numbers and the spending of United Kingdom residents who take trips to different parts of the country, the following information could be used:

Trips by United Kingdom residents to England and regions, January to June 2000–2002

	All trips Jan to June 2000 (Millions)	All trips Jan to June 2001 (Millions)	All trips Jan to June 2002 (Millions)	Percentage change 2002 v 2001	Percentage change 2002 v 2000
ENGLAND	64.9	55.5	63.0	14	−3
Cumbria	2.3	1.8	1.8	0	−22
Northumbria	2.7	1.8	2.4	33	−11
North West	7.0	5.9	6.4	8	−9
Yorkshire	6.0	4.4	5.8	32	−3
Heart of England	11.7	9.5	11.5	21	−2
East of England	6.2	5.3	6.7	26	8
London	9.1	7.7	8.0	4	−12
South West	7.8	7.8	9.2	18	18
Southern	6.4	5.1	6.9	35	8
South East	4.8	5.6	5.1	−9	6

Source: United Kingdom Tourism Survey

Expenditure of United Kingdom residents taking trips to England and regions, January to June 2000–2002

	All trips Jan to June 2000 (£ millions)	All trips Jan to June 2001 (£ millions)	All trips Jan to June 2002 (£ millions)	Percentage change 2002 v 2001	Percentage change 2002 v 2000
ENGLAND	8413	7936	9392.0	18	12
Cumbria	304	259	281.0	8	−8
Northumbria	357	213	479.8	125	34
North West	856	855	1018.7	19	19
Yorkshire	733	512	749.6	46	2
Heart of England	1346	1139	1471.2	29	9
East of England	653	674	783.4	16	20
London	1449	1413	1338.2	−5	−8
South West	1122	1184	1485.6	25	32
Southern	736	735	976.9	33	33
South East	558	675	605.7	−10	9

Source: United Kingdom Tourism Survey

Wales

Yorkshire

Cornwall

FIND IT OUT

Which is the most popular area of England for United Kingdom tourists? What is 'the Heart of England'? Name at least five towns and cities and three tourist attractions in the region. If a business was thinking of setting up a tourist attraction, such as a theme park in a part of England, which area offers the least in terms of visitors and money spent?

Budgets and time

Leisure and tourism businesses often cannot afford to spend vast amounts of money conducting market research. Market research costs could be large and these could cut into profits. Normally, both market research and the general marketing effort (including advertising and other promotions) will be given a fixed percentage of income. This means that money has to be well spent and also has to provide obvious benefits to the business and its products and services. This is usually measured in terms of increases in the number of customers, visitors to an attraction or the amount of products and services sold. If the market research does not reveal useful information that the business can act upon, then the money that was spent is likely to be considered to have been wasted.

Alongside the problem of getting value for money from market research, there is also the time factor. If a market research study takes too long to collect and analyse the data, then the information may well be out of date before it is ready to be looked at. Like many things, if a leisure and tourism business decides to do some market research then it wants it today! By the time it has decided why it wants the information and how to collect it and analyse it many months may have passed.

There are two ways to cut down on the time – either to employ professionals to collect the information for you and to analyse it and then present you with a finished report, or to do the research yourself. Using professionals does cut down the time but the costs of the research will be high. The other alternative, to do the research yourself, will be cheaper, but unless people in the organisation have some experience of carrying out research it may take much longer and they may miss vital pieces of information.

Think IT THROUGH

What kind of information would a leisure centre have about the type of customers who use the facility? Where would this information be stored? How could it add to the information to get a clearer picture of its customers?

The market research process should follow these clear steps in order to make sure that the research does what is required of it and that it is of value when finished. Here are the key steps of the process:

Stage of the process	Details of the stage
Pre-research planning	The business clearly states what the research is for and what decisions will be helped by it.
Technical specifications	The business needs to decide how many people will be interviewed or sent questionnaires (this is called a sample). This is where cost and time factors are considered.
Questionnaire development	The questionnaire now needs to be designed. It is a good idea to test out the questionnaire before it is used. Any lesson learned from this test will mean that the questionnaire may have to be redesigned.
Data collection	A business or a market research company would make spot checks on whether the data is being collected properly. Once the questionnaires have been collected in, they need to be checked to see that the customer has completed all of the questions.
Data processing	This is when the results of the questionnaires are brought together and the answers are added up or noted so that they form the basis of the report. Figures need to add up correctly (make sure that percentages total 100% and so forth).
Reporting results	The data now need to be analysed and the main points put in a summary (in a lot of cases businesses only ever read this summary and not the full report). Recommendations need to be put forward from the information collected (and a business would also want plans to put these recommendations into practice). The researchers would present the report as a paper-based document and make an oral presentation to the decision makers in the business.

What does a report look like? What are the headings in a report? See if you can find a report template in Microsoft® Word; which format would you choose?

FIND IT OUT

Methods

Having looked at the research process we now need to turn our attention to the ways of collecting the information needed.

There are several different ways to collect information during market research. Let us begin by looking at the differences between the main types of data collection:

Comparison of telephone, personal, mail, email and Internet survey

Key points	Telephone	Personal	Mail	Email	Internet
Ability to handle complex questions	Good	Excellent	Poor	Poor	Poor
Ability to collect large amounts of data from customer	Good	Excellent	Fair	Fair	Fair
Accuracy on sensitive questions	Fair	Fair	Good	Good	Good
Control of interviewer effects	Good	Poor	Good	Good	Good
Ability to make sure sample is accurate	Good	Excellent	Poor	Good	Fair
Time required	Excellent	Fair	Poor	Excellent	Good
Probable response rate	Good	Fair	Fair	Fair	Fair
Cost	Good	Poor	Good	Excellent	Good
Ability to ensure questionnaire completion	Poor	Excellent	Excellent	Good	Good

Postal surveys

Postal surveys (questionnaires sent out by mail) are often used by a business or a market research company to obtain information from customers. The people who are sent questionnaires and fill them in are called respondents. Here are the strengths and weaknesses of postal surveys:

Strengths of postal questionnaires	Weaknesses of postal questionnaires
Relatively easy and inexpensive to set up and control	Not many respondents bother to fill in the questionnaire and sent it back
Respondents can give thoughtful and considered responses	You cannot be sure that the person the questionnaire was sent to actually filled it in
Respondents have the time to think about their answers	Sending out the questionnaires and waiting for them to return can be a long period of time
There is no interviewer involved, so respondents actually put down what they think and not what they think the interviewer wants to hear	Because there is no one there to thank them for bothering, the respondents might not feel that their opinions actually matter
It does not matter where the respondent is – the questionnaires can be mailed to anyone, anywhere	Respondents can read through the questionnaires first and choose answers that mean that they don't need to fill in later parts of the questionnaire

Think IT THROUGH

How might a leisure and tourism business collect addresses that could be used to send out a postal survey? From where do you think they would obtain this information?

Telephone questionnaires

Telephone questionnaires need more time and trained staff. The person making the call to the customer reads the questions as well as a possible range of answers. Here are the strengths and weaknesses of telephone interviews:

Strengths of telephone interviews	Weaknesses of telephone interviews
The quickest method of data collection – the answers can be typed straight into a database	The pace of interview is usually fast, reducing thinking time
Inexpensive	Time pressure can affect the quality of the interview
Problems with questionnaire design can be dealt with quickly	No opportunity to see the respondents or where they live or work
Telephone interviews can be carried out with respondents living in many different parts of the country or the world	Respondents may fear that the call is not really market research and that the caller is trying to sell them something
People are quite happy (usually) to talk on the telephone	The interviewer may have to hurry the respondent up and suggest answers if they take too much time
Respondents are most likely to reply to a phone call ahead of any other method	The researcher may not hear the answer properly because of a poor line or the fact that the respondent's voice is not clear

Personal surveys

Personal surveys are also known as face-to-face or personal interviews. This involves actually asking the respondent in person in the street or their workplace. It can be a very useful way of collecting information for market research. Here are the strengths and weaknesses of personal interviews:

case study

Wildlife tourism in the Minch

The Minch is a part of the Western Isles of Scotland. Scottish Natural Heritage, Comhairle nan Eilean and others have been involved in the Minch Project. As part of this, a number of works were commissioned, one of which was a project on wildlife tourism.

Thirty-five operators of short boat trips in the area were interviewed by telephone (out of a total of 36 identified). Most of these trips are of a general nature and do not focus exclusively on wildlife. Virtually every vessel used for short boat trips is powered by motor; 49% of the trips are operated on a regular, daily basis (weather permitting); 43% of the operators take part in other activities such as diving and angling. For these operators, general cruises are undertaken only on demand; 55% of the trips have been in existence for less than five years; 92% of the trips operate between the months of April and October only. The length of the trips ranges from less than one hour to all day; 57% of the trips last between one and three hours. The price per trip ranges from £0 to £25; 51% of the trips cost between £5 and £10; 49% of the trips allow tourists to disembark at some point in the journey; 80% of the operators have alternative sources of income, both during and out of season.

Q1 *Do you think that the number of people interviewed by telephone was sufficient to get decent results for the research? State your reasons.*

Q2 *Why do you think that the researchers chose to carry out the interviews by telephone?*

Q3 *What is the season for the trips? What is the average price per person charged for the trips and how long do they last?*

Q4 *Whale watching is one of the big attractions in the area. Visit the Western Isles website (www.w-isles.gov.uk) and find out at least five other areas that are supporting tourism.*

Strengths of personal interviews	Weaknesses of personal interviews
The interviewer helps respondents by prompting and encouraging them	The cost of transportation to and from the interview
The interviewer can see the respondents' reactions	The travelling time to the interview
The respondent has time to think and give better answers	There is a risk that the interviewer might suggest answers
Respondents can be interviewed in their own surroundings	Organising personal interviews across the country can be difficult and expensive
Respondents will give the interviewer their full attention during the interview	It is often difficult for the interviewer to be sure that the respondent is the right sort of person needed for the survey

Can you just conduct personal interviews anywhere? Do you need permission from the council or the police? Can you ask people to answer questionnaires outside a shop? Do you need permission from the shop owner or manager? Your local council or local police would be able to tell you the answers to these questions.

FIND IT OUT

Observation

Observation research could be very useful for leisure and tourism organisations. The techniques include the following:

- mystery shopping – using people posing as customers to see how the employees handle queries and complaints;

- mystery calling – using people posing as customers to make calls to the organisation to see how their problems or queries are handled;

- visitor flow analysis – choosing an individual customer or group of customers and following them inside the attraction to see where they go, how long they spend in each area and what they buy;

- general observation – watching customers and seeing what interests them either in a shop or at an attraction

(this may be done using cameras set up at points around the site).

A leisure and tourism organisation could use observation to collect information about the following areas:

- Environment and facilities – is everything working properly, clean and tidy, well presented?
- Service standards – are specific standards being met, all the time, every time?
- Politeness and helpfulness of staff – do staff have good skills with the customers?
- Product knowledge – do staff understand the features, functions and benefits of the products/services offered?
- Procedures knowledge – staff may know what to do, but do they know how?
- Test purchases – do staff sell effectively?
- Refunds and complaints procedures – how are customers treated when returning products and how are customer complaints handled?
- Product support – are new products being promoted effectively?
- Promotional materials – are sales leaflets and brochures being displayed effectively?
- Helplines, support lines – how well does the business perform when dealing with customers on the telephone?
- Price audits – are prices competitive?
- Legal checks – are staff observing laws and the business's own recommended safety checks?
- Websites – how well does the business perform when dealing with customers online?

FIND IT OUT

How would you feel if you knew that you were being observed either as an employee or a customer? Would it bother you? Briefly explain your views on this.

What might a mystery shopper be asked to do? Have a look at www.beamysteryshopper.co.uk *and see if you can find out what is required.*

Email and Internet

In addition to surveying by the usual methods such as postal or telephone questionnaires there has been a growing trend in online surveying. Many websites, belonging to both commercial and public organisations, carry questionnaires that can be completed online.

Strengths of email research	Weaknesses of email research
Visual images may be used to make the questionnaire more interesting	It is not possible to know who actually completed the questionnaire
Very low cost	If the answer is not clear, there is no chance to follow up with another question to make it clearer
Very little time required to set up	Only those interested may reply
It is easy to see how many questionnaires are coming back, more can be sent if needed	Cannot reach everyone – only those with email access
Respondents can complete the questionnaire on their own	Email filters (which stop unwanted emails) may prevent the email getting through
If the questionnaire can be filled in without stating your name, the respondent may answer personal questions	The research relies on being able to obtain the email addresses in the first place

Using the Internet to collect market research information offers two different methods: email research and Internet (or website research). Email research is just like a more modern method of a postal survey. The questionnaire is emailed to the respondents and they email it back. Internet research involves putting the questionnaire on a website and hoping that people will spend the time to fill it in.

Strengths of Internet research	Weaknesses of Internet research
Audio and visual aids may be used	You need to find out where respondents live to see whether what they are saying is useful
Respondents can complete the questionnaire on their own	If the answer is not clear, there is no chance to follow up with another question to make it clearer
Respondents may answer personal questions if the questionnaire can be filled in without them stating their names	Only those who are interested may answer the questionnaire
Fast way of obtaining data	Cannot reach everyone; only those with Internet access
Can be used for anyone who visits a website or just for those that have registered with the website	It is not possible to know who actually completed the questionnaire
Respondents do answer personal questions	Only those that have found the website may take time to fill in the questionnaire
Respondents can be asked whether they would help with further research	There may be a long period before enough respondents have completed the questionnaire

Questionnaire design

A questionnaire is an ideal way of collecting information about customers. A questionnaire is a set of questions either written (the customer fills out the question on paper) or verbal (the interviewer asks the questions and writes down the customer's answers).

A good questionnaire design should mean that the customer can answer all of the questions accurately and provide the business with useful information.

It is not always easy to design a questionnaire correctly. Care needs to be given to how questions are phrased. This goes not only for the question, but also the possible answers. Here are some key thoughts on questionnaire design:

- Decide what it is you want to find out (this may sound obvious, but not all questionnaires seem to have a purpose).
- Choose a question type or series of question types (we will look at this later) and think about how you are going to add up the scores or categorise the answers. This needs to be as simple as possible.

Email market research

case study

In December 2002, around 2500 emails were sent to holidaymakers. Two segments were chosen: those that had been on a package holiday and those that had been on another type of holiday. The response rate was 15%.

The market research company TARP was interested in customer loyalty and discovered that many of the holidaymakers were less than satisfied about the levels of service given to them by the tour companies.

The main points of the study found that around 50% of the respondents were very satisfied and of these 73% would rebook and 83% would recommend the tour operator to others.

Around 30% of the respondents had had problems with their holiday and of these only 20% would rebook.

The biggest problem was the way in which the tour operators' staff handled complaints. Some 85% said that they were not happy with the way in which their complaints were dealt with. Around 65% of those that complained on holiday contacted the resort rep and 86% said that the rep did not handle their complaints very well.

The survey estimated that £286 million was being lost each year by customers not rebooking as a result of having been given poor customer service and their complaints not being handled professionally.

Source: adapted from information from TARP www.tarp.co.uk.

Q1 *If TARP sent out 2500 emails and received 15% back, how many questionnaires were actually completed?*

Q2 *Were holidaymakers that had a problem on holiday more or less likely to send back a completed questionnaire? Give reasons for your decision.*

Q3 *If you were a tour operator, suggest three things you might do as a result of finding out this information.*

- Choose the question type that will give you the information that you are looking for. Remember that the way questions are phrased will change the way people respond.

- Think about how the customer is going to answer the question. Are you going to give them options (which makes it easier to analyse the responses later) or are you going to let the customers answer in their own words (which might be harder to analyse)?

- Now choose the exact wording of the questions. Will the customers understand exactly what you are asking them?

- Now make sure the order of the questions is logical. If you are asking questions like name, age and address, don't scatter them around in the questionnaire – have them all together.

- Work out how many questions you can fit on to a page – make sure there's room to put the answers, but not too much space otherwise customers might think you are expecting them to write an essay each time!

- Make sure that you test the questionnaire and revise it as needed.

Before you give out any of the questionnaires, figure out how you are going to analyse them. Draw up some tables on a computer. You can use these to mark each answer in the right box and speed up your analysis.

The types of questions you can ask will either help you or hinder you in finding out what the results are and will make the customer's job harder or easier. We consider 'open' and 'closed' types of questions a little later but for now here are some options about question types:

- Questions that offer multiple-choice answers. These types of questions are good when the possible replies are few and clear cut, such as age or the number of times an activity is done.

Example

Please state your age:

Under 16 ☑   17–19 ☐   20–25 ☐   26–30 ☐   31–40 ☐   41+ ☐

Make your own multiple choice question, based on the one above, for your local leisure centre asking people to mark the sports or activities they take part in at the centre.

FIND IT OUT

- Open-ended questions allow customers to better express their answer but are more difficult to administer and analyse. Open-ended questions mean that you just leave a blank after the question. Don't forget that this type of question is harder to analyse because the person answering can say anything.

Example

Please tell us what other facilities or activities you would like us to develop at the centre.

....

....

If you were to design a questionnaire and had an open-ended question like this, how would you sort the answers? What would you do if the person completed the question and had several suggestions and not just one?

Think IT THROUGH

- The questionnaire could use word associations and fill-in-the-blank sentences. These are difficult to analyse and probably not a good idea if you want basic information.

Example
Please complete the following sentences with your own words:

Overall I _____ my visit to the theme park today. I _____ come to the park again. My favourite ride was _____ and my least favourite was _____ .

Design your own series of fill-in-the-blank sentences for a leisure or tourism facility. Make sure that the person can be positive or negative and that the sentences will make sense no matter what the person puts into the blanks.

There are other options and using these gives you the chance to make the questionnaire look a little more interesting and exciting:

- Graphic questions – the customer simply makes a mark on a line between two extremes. Customers can mark the line anywhere they want but this is difficult to analyse.

Example
How would you rate your day's visit here?
Excellent ◄─────────────────────────► Very disappointing

- Itemised questions – quite similar to graphic questions except there are a limited number of places along the line that can be marked.

Example

How would you rate your day's visit here?

Excellent   Very good   Good   OK   Disappointing   Not good   Poor

---

- Comparative questions – the customer is asked to compare the product or service with another known product or service and asked to state what is better or worse.

Example

Please compare and rate our following services (please underline your choice):

Our own brand cola with Coca-Cola or Pepsi	Better	Same	Worse
Our speed of service with KFC	Better	Same	Worse
Our cleanliness with McDonald's	Better	Same	Worse

Don't forget that there should be a reason for each question in the questionnaire or you shouldn't have it in at all. The only purpose of the questions is to obtain the information you need.

Depending on the types of questions you ask you can get very different types of answers:

- open-ended questions will give you open-ended answers that are difficult to analyse;
- a straightforward question that just requires the customer to answer 'yes' or 'no' can be easy to analyse, but doesn't actually tell you much;
- multiple-choice questions are useful as they can offer the customer a range of answers and are still quite easy to analyse;
- getting the wording right in the questionnaires is the hardest trick but you need to be careful and take time in thinking them through – make sure you try them out on people before you finally decide on the wording.

Good and bad wording of questions

'Which cinema do you use?' might seem clear at first, but who is 'you'? The person you are asking the question? That person's family? When do you mean? What about how often? What about the other cinemas used? Are you asking the customer to tell you the name of the last cinema or the most used cinema? Better wording might be: 'Which cinema have you used personally during the past six months? If you have used more than one cinema, please list each of them.'

Now you are asking about how often – and the customers are clear that it just means them. If you wanted to follow up this question with another question like, 'How often have you visited the cinema in the past six months?' you need to discourage respondents from giving you vague answers such as 'regularly' or 'occasionally'. Give them options like 'once a month', 'every week', 'only once or twice'.

Even simple things like the font and font size that you use can have an effect on the way customers will answer your questionnaires. If the questionnaire is hard to read they won't bother. If they think that it will take too long they won't bother. The trick is to get them to complete the questionnaire and give you the information that you need – so make it easy for them.

Think IT THROUGH

How many questions or pages do you think it is reasonable to ask a person to complete? Do you think that having very different types of questions will keep the person interested?

How leisure and tourism organisations carry out market research

Typically, the leisure and tourism industry will carry out the following research related to customers:

- customer satisfaction studies – how satisfied customers are with the business;
- customer care programmes – how well the business looks after its customers;

- identification of customer types – the typical customer of the business;
- exit/in-store interviews – face-to-face interviews that take place in the facility or at the attraction while the customer is there or just leaving;
- shopping habits/patterns research – looking at how often a customer visits the facility or the attraction and what they buy once they are there;
- loyalty/store card surveys – discovering whether customers would like to be offered a card, or in the case of facilities or attractions that have one already whether the customer makes full use of the benefits offered;
- lifestyle/shopping studies – general surveys that look at particular segments to investigate their habits;
- pricing and expenditure surveys – how the costs of the facility or the attraction compare with the competitors and what people are spending their money on at the moment;
- competitor analysis – looking at the closest competitors (these may be geographically close or offer similar products or services);
- catchment area studies – looking at the population in the immediate area of the facility or the attraction – this may use a number of different segmentation categories;
- reactions to improvements – finding out what the customers think of a facility or attraction after the business has spent time and money on improving it, compared to what they thought of it before;
- communications research – discovering what customers know about the facility or the attraction from the advertising and other marketing activities of the business.

Look at the list of different types of research above. Which types of research are the following?

- *A leisure centre wants to know how many 16 to 25 year olds there are within five miles of the centre.*
- *A theme park wants to know whether their entrance prices are reasonable compared to other parks.*
- *A travel agent is thinking about offering discount cards to regular customers.*

The marketing mix

What is the marketing mix?

The marketing mix is the balance of the 'four Ps' used by an organisation. Each leisure and tourism business will have a different balance of the 'four Ps' – their own marketing mix, which works for them. In other words, different leisure and tourism businesses have different products and services to offer to different customers.

They offer these to different groups of people, which they have identified as being ideal customers from their market research and experience. They also charge different prices, perhaps changing the prices according to the time of year or the popularity of the product or service. Their products or services are also available in different places – the more places you can buy the product or the service, the more customers you may have.

Finally, different businesses have different ways of promoting their products or services. Some use newspaper advertisements, some use the television. Others may choose advertisements on websites and others may print leaflets or pay for posters to be put up at railway stations or along roads. Each leisure and tourism business will try to find the best way of promoting its products and services in order to attract the maximum number of customers. As we will see, this choice is very important because you want the people that are or may be your customers to be able to hear about you.

FIND IT OUT

Using the Internet and your local Yellow Pages, list at least 10 different places where you could buy a ticket for a flight to Rome with British Airways. Include five online 'places' and five 'places' you can go in and buy the ticket in person.

The 'four Ps'

The 'four Ps' of the marketing mix cover many of the choices and activities of marketing. These are:

- product (what goods and services an organisation offers);
- price (how much the goods and services cost);
- place (where the goods and services are offered);
- promotion (how organisations get people to buy their goods and services).

Let's look at the 'four Ps' in a little more detail.

Product

A product is anything offered for sale or use. Products can be physical objects, services, people, places, organisations and ideas.

You will sometimes hear the phrase 'goods and services'. This is just another way of saying 'product'. A Sony PlayStation, a visit to Alton Towers, a Pizza Hut meal, an Avis car for hire, advice from a fitness instructor, and a holiday package to the Greek Islands are all products. Services are products that consist of activities, benefits or satisfactions that are offered for sale.

Product or service features

A useful way of thinking about the features of a product or a service is to look at the product or service as a broader package. This package includes the product itself, what it is called, how it looks and additional considerations such as after-sales service. These are known as *product levels* and they are best understood in the following diagram:

THE JARGON DRAGON

core product – the basic product or service, for example a holiday, a day out or entertainment

actual product – the way in which the core product is presented to the customer (a package holiday, a theme park or a movie at a cinema)

tangible product – something physical that customers can take away with them such as a baseball cap, a stick of rock or a programme

intangible service – something that customers buy but cannot take away with them, such as a day in a theme park, an aerobics class or flight

augmented product – everything that is not to do with the product or the service but makes it easier for the customer to buy and to take the decision to buy, such as paying in instalments for a holiday, knowing that a product has a guarantee or even that the business where they made their purchase has a good reputation for dealing with problems

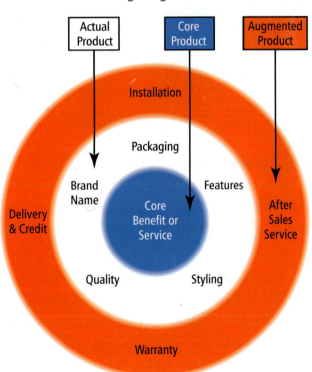

- The **core product** – what the buyer is really buying. The core product refers to the use, benefit or problem-solving service that the customer is really buying when purchasing the product – in other words the need that is being fulfilled. When you buy a holiday package, the core products are the flight and the accommodation.
- The **actual product** is the **tangible product** or **intangible service** that allows the customer to receive the core-product benefits. So the actual product is a holiday package, which is the flight tickets and the services of the company to get you from the airport to the accommodation and vice versa.
- *Quality* refers to product performance – how many attractions there are at a theme park, whether the hotel was as described in the brochure or whether the flight left on time.

FIND IT OUT

Choose a leisure or tourism product or service. Draw your own version of the diagram opposite and replace the labels in the diagram with your own description of that product or service. Does the product or service have all the features on the diagram? What is the core product? What is the actual product? Where do quality, features, style and packaging come in?

- *Features* are the product attributes – what it does and what it is for.
- *Styling* refers to the design of the product – how it is made to appear to the customer.
- The *brand name* helps consumers recognise the product and judge whether it has a good reputation.
- *Packaging* protects tangible products from damage. It also helps to promote both products and services by featuring the style and the brand name.
- The **augmented product** consists of things made available to help the customer make an easier choice. It helps to convince the customer that it is the product that they should buy, including **installation**, **delivery** and **credit**, **warranties**, and **after-sales service**.

A product is more than a simple set of tangible features. Customers tend to see products and services as being a bundle of benefits that satisfy their needs.

Brand name

A brand name is an important part of a product and branding can make the product all that more appealing to customers. A brand name is the name by which customers know the product or service. Examples of brand names include Nike, Reebok, Alton Towers or British Airways London Eye. Let's look at brand names and branding in a little more detail:

- Branding allows a business to describe its products or services in such a way that customers instantly recognise it.
- Owning a major brand name means that customers automatically know whether the product or the service is

THE JARGON DRAGON

installation – in the case of products such as satellite dishes or cable TV this is normally done by a professional who does the work for the customer

delivery – when customers can expect to receive what they have ordered

credit – allowing the customer to spread the cost of paying for products and services over a period of time (this may convince a customer who is not sure about buying to think again)

warranties (guarantees) – the business guarantees that the product or service will do what the business claims it will do, otherwise customers may be able to get their money back

MARKS & SPENCER

worth buying. The more that is spent on promoting the brand the better it is known and the better the reputation it might have.

- Many businesses have spent millions of pounds promoting their brands. They include companies such as Thomson Holidays, Madam Tussaud's, BlockBuster Video and Nike. Once the brand has become established in the minds of the customers, many are loyal to it and regularly buy products and services from the business that owns it.

- Once the brand has become strong, the business does not need to worry too much about the competition. It does not need to cut prices because customers are loyal to it. Customers actually prefer to buy the brand even if the competitors are cheaper.

Think
IT THROUGH

Think about some other brand names. Can you list five related to the leisure industry and five related to travel or tourism? How do you know about them? Think about where you heard the name first.

After-sales service

THE JARGON DRAGON

after-sales service – customer service after the customer has bought the product or the service, including support and information as well as dealing with queries and complaints

You might think that **after-sales service** only refers to tangible products that might be faulty at some point after the customer has bought them. After-sales service is far more complicated than that and is a very important part of customer service.

When a customer buys a product or a service and has parted with money for it this should not be the end of the organisation's involvement with the customer. The organisation wants customers to be completely happy with what they have bought. So any problems after the sale has been made will be dealt with. Good after-sales service means that customers will have more confidence in buying from that organisation again.

> Look at the four examples of after-sales service problems below and choose one of them. Write a short letter or jot down what you might say to the person described in each case.
>
> - A person who has visited a zoo discovers that she has lost her purse.
> - A person who flew to Paris with an airline discovered that some items in his luggage had been damaged in transit.
> - A person who purchased a souvenir programme of his visit to a museum found that when he arrived home two of the pages are blank.
> - A person who visited a theme park that said it had plenty of rides for her young children found that they only spent half a day there as the few rides were too busy.

FIND IT OUT

Product life cycle

Imagine a product or a service as being a living creature. It is born (launched), grows, reaches maturity and eventually slips into decline. This is also a useful way to look at how popular the product or service is over a period of time. The major difference between a product or service's life cycle is that it can be very short or last for many years – it all depends on how popular it remains and how successful the business that offers it remains over time. For example in the leisure industry, activities such as keeping fit have changed over the years as trends have come and gone. It seems that nearly all TV and pop personalities produce their own video of how to keep fit and healthy. However, keeping fit still remains popular, no matter how it is dressed up. Other leisure activities, such as dry-ski slopes, skateboard parks and roller skating rinks pass in and out of popularity and have short product life cycles. It is also useful to look at the product life cycle and consider what is happening to the 'four Ps' along the way.

Here is a typical product life cycle: 'time' is how long the life lasts and 'sales' refers to the popularity of the product over that time.

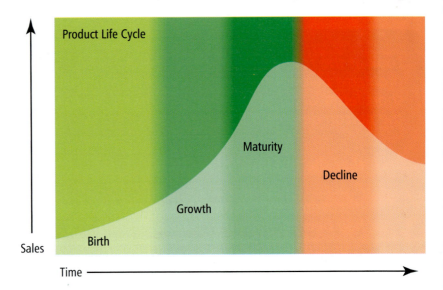

Birth or introduction stage

In the birth or introduction stage, the business hopes to build **product awareness** and develop a market for the product. The impact on the marketing mix is as follows:

- **product** branding and quality level is established;
- **pricing** may be low to build **market share** rapidly;
- **place (distribution)** is selective (only available in certain places) until customers show acceptance of the product;
- **promotion** is aimed at those willing to try something out before most other people. Promotion seeks to build product awareness and to educate potential customers about the product. At this stage the amount of promotion is high.

Growth stage

In the growth stage, the business seeks to build **brand preference** and increase market share.

- **product** quality is maintained and additional features and support services may be added;
- **pricing** is maintained as the business enjoys increasing demand with little competition;

THE JARGON DRAGON

product awareness – the process of telling potential customers that the product or service exists

market share – the amount of a business's products and services sold as a percentage of the total number of products and services sold by all competing businesses

- **place (distribution)** channels are added as demand increases and customers accept the product;
- **promotion** is aimed at a broader audience.

Maturity stage

At maturity, the strong growth in sales slows down. Competition may appear with similar products. Marketing efforts now switch to defending market share while **maximising profit**:

- **product** features may be improved to show that the product is different and better from that of competitors;
- **pricing** may be lower because of the new competition;
- **distribution** becomes more widespread and discounts may be offered to encourage customers to choose the product over competing products;
- **promotion** focuses on the differences and quality of the product;
- **people** – market research looks at what customers would like to be improved and the features of competitors' products and services.

Decline stage

As sales decline, the business has several options:

- maintain the product, possibly by adding new features and finding new uses;
- try to reduce costs and continue to offer it, possibly to a loyal segment;
- **discontinue** the product, selling off any remaining stock (if it is a product) or selling it to another business that is willing to continue the product.

THE JARGON DRAGON

brand preference – which brand the majority of customers like to use

maximising profit – trying to make as much money as possible by cutting down on costs

discontinue – stop offering a product or service to customers

Price

Most leisure and tourism businesses must set a price for their products and services. This is certainly true of organisations that are concerned with making a profit. Many leisure and tourism organisations, such as tourist information centres, do not set prices on their services as such – they receive the money they need to operate from local councils and other sources.

Price is the only part of the marketing mix that actually produces an income for the business; all of the other parts of the marketing mix represent a cost. Price is the amount of money that is charged to the customer for a product or a service – it is the price that customers pay to receive the benefit of the service or for owning the product.

Price is also the most flexible part of the marketing mix. Prices can be changed quickly. Even short-term price changes can be made, such as offering discounts. Price is normally based on the following:

- the amount of money it costs the business to provide a service or buy a product (plus, of course, some extra so that the business can make a profit);
- the price is also often based on what customers are prepared to pay – too high a price compared with prices that have been paid might mean that customers stop buying;
- the price will also be based on what the competition is charging – too high a price will mean that the competition takes most of the customers and too low may make the customers think that what is being offered is not very good quality.

Price is extremely important as it is often this that makes a customer decide whether or not to buy. No matter how successful all of the other parts of the marketing mix have been, a high price will scare off customers.

In recent years, however, customers have been looking for products and services that offer more than just good value for money. Many customers now place quality above price, but this does not mean that they are prepared to pay very high prices just to receive the quality that they demand.

Actual selling price

You may have noticed that many businesses have two prices. One may be called the 'recommended retail price' or the 'manufacturer's recommended price'. The other is the actual price. You may also see, particularly in travel agents and in tour operators' brochures, that two prices are mentioned. One will be high, but the real price that you are expected to pay will be lower. The brochure may tell you, '20% off if you book before April' or 'one child goes free with every two adults'.

Pricing strategies usually change as the product passes through its life cycle, as we have seen. Businesses that offer a brand new product or service have to set the price without the benefit of knowing what a customer might pay or what the competition is charging. This is when market research can help in setting the price by finding out what customers may be prepared to pay.

Think
IT THROUGH

Are there new leisure or tourism businesses opening or that have just opened in your area? Are they offering lower introductory prices? Why might they offer these lower prices for the first few weeks to customers?

When a business adds a product or a service, it also needs to decide on the prices to set, and product features to offer to make sure that the customers recognise it as a different product or service from what was on offer before.

Theatres and sports teams sell season tickets where the cost of an individual event in the season ticket bundle is less than the normal cost of a ticket for a single event. Hotels sell specially priced packages that include a room, meals and entertainment. Restaurants offer complete dinner menu bundles that are cheaper than selecting the same individual items from the *à la carte* menu. This is known as price bundling and it can promote the sale of products that customers might not otherwise buy, but the combined price must be low enough to encourage them to buy the bundle.

Credit terms

Credit terms are not often relevant for most leisure and tourism products and services such as a day's ticket for a theme park, using a local swimming pool or buying a meal in a restaurant. The customer can, in most cases, use a **credit card** to pay for the product or service, but these are not, strictly speaking, credit terms offered by the business itself.

Credit terms are slightly more complicated and are usually relevant to purchases of higher value and are designed so that the customer can spread the cost of the product or service over a period of time.

Examples of credit terms in the leisure and tourism industry include:

- a leisure centre or health club allowing customers to pay a monthly subscription fee (membership fee) instead of paying the full yearly amount when they join;
- a travel agency allowing customers to pay a deposit when they book the holiday and the balance several weeks before they take the holiday.

THE JARGON DRAGON

credit terms – offering the customer the opportunity to pay for a product or service over a longer period of time instead of paying the full amount at once

credit card – issued to a customer by a bank or building society, it allows the customer to spend money and pay a percentage of the money they owe on a monthly basis. This helps the customer to spread the costs of expensive purchases.

Visit a local health club and find out what the credit terms are on membership. Do they offer monthly payments? How does the customer pay these monthly payments? Do they pay more than they would have paid if they had made the full payment when they joined?

Profitability

As we have seen, price is the only part of the marketing mix that allows the business to have any chance of making a profit. The business needs to be able to work out its costs and set a price that allows it to make a profit from selling the products and services that it offers. In other words, the business needs to work out exactly how much it costs to offer the product or service (including wages, costs of their premises, advertising and other costs), then add a percentage to make a profit.

This is not as easy as it might sound because costs can change and it is difficult to work out exactly how much something cost in the first place. Here is an example, just to illustrate how complicated it can become. This is a simple version of what it might involve for a theme park:

COSTS

Daily wages paid – £10 000 (total wage bill divided by 365).

Daily electricity – £5000 (total electricity bill divided by 365).

Daily repairs – £4000 (total repair bill divided by 365).

Daily advertising – £5000 (total advertising bill divided by 365).

Total – £24 000 (yearly total cost is £876 000).

Suppose that the theme park attracts (to make the calculations easier) 87 600 people each year. It would need to charge £10 entrance fee to cover its costs. The problem is that the costs listed above are not the only things that the theme park has to pay for each year. A new ride could cost it £2 million or staff training could cost it £500 000. This added cost of £2.5 million pushes up the yearly costs to £3 376 000, which means that the 87 600 people visiting the theme park would now have to pay £38.50 just for the theme park to cover its costs. A huge increase in entrance price would not be acceptable to customers and far fewer people would come.

Think IT THROUGH

Think about the example above. How would the theme park pay for the new ride? Would it pass the whole of the cost on to their customers in one year? Can you think of other costs that a theme park might have? What other products and services does it sell to make money and more profit?

Place

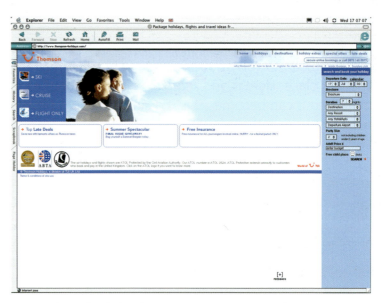

Place includes all of the business activities involved in making the product available to target consumers. Place means making the product or service convenient for the target customers to purchase.

For an airline, this would cover all of the travel agents, websites and other places where customers could buy tickets for their flights. For a cinema, place would include the cinema itself, online booking and buying tickets on the telephone. A hotel, for example, may have several different places where customers could book rooms; perhaps the rooms are available as part of a holiday package offered by a tour operator through its own brochures and website as well as through travel agents. Hotel rooms may also be available from the hotel's own website.

> *Find the name of a hotel featured in a holiday brochure where accommodation is included in the package price. Using the Internet, try to find the website of the hotel and see if you can book accommodation with it directly.*

The important aspect of 'place' is making the product or service as widely available as possible. The more places in which it is available, the more likely it is that customers will hear about it and will be able to buy it.

> *Choose a local hotel and search for its name on the Internet. Note down how many different places offer to sell you rooms for the hotel. What facilities does the hotel offer its customers?*

Types of outlet or facility used (channels of distribution)

Most businesses use **intermediaries** to bring their products to market. They try to create a distribution channel in making goods and services available to target markets.

Normal channel of distribution

Travel and tourism version of channel of distribution

THE JARGON DRAGON

intermediaries – other businesses that sell products and services on behalf of another business (such as a travel agent selling holidays for a tour operator)

THE JARGON DRAGON

scale of operations – the number of outlets and the size of the business, such as the number of travel agency shops in a chain across the country

Although turning over part of the selling to intermediaries means giving up some control over how and to whom products are sold, leisure and tourism businesses know that the use of these specialists results in greater efficiency and higher sales. Through their contacts, experience and **scale of operations**, intermediaries usually offer the business more than it can achieve on its own.

Intermediaries may be able to sell more products and services than the business would be able to sell if it just offered its products and services itself. It does mean that the intermediaries need to be paid a percentage of each sale made and that, overall, the business does not make as much profit on each product or service sold – but it does sell more.

Location of outlets and facilities

New leisure and tourism outlets and facilities are usually built where there is a large local population, but there are many other factors that determine where a facility might be located:

- the site may be located near to good transport routes;
- the site may have to be located in an area that has particular features (such as by a river for canoeing or in an area which has snow for skiing);
- the site may be already there, in the case of a historical site such as a castle or an old building;
- the site may have to be chosen because the land is the only site available in the area;
- the site may be chosen because the area is already attracting large numbers of visitors.

Think
IT THROUGH

Think of at least three other reasons why an outlet or a facility might be located where it is.

?

Identification of distribution channels

Distribution channels perform many key functions that help to complete the transaction between the seller and the buyer.

They perform the following tasks:

- information gathering and distributing marketing research and intelligence about market trends;
- promotion and development of communications about the product or service to customers;
- contact and finding customers;
- matching customers' needs with the products or services available;
- negotiation in reaching an agreement on price and other terms (such as credit) with the customer;
- physical distribution of a product, including transporting and storing goods;
- risk taking in stocking products.

THE JARGON DRAGON

distribution channels move goods from producers to consumers – they overcome the major time and place gaps that separate goods and services from those who would use them

Suggest the distribution channels for the following leisure and tourism products and services. Identify the stages and organisations involved in the process.

- *A ticket to see the FA Cup Final, including travel to Cardiff.*
- *A ride on the British Airways London Eye.*
- *A guided tour on a bus or coach around the sights of London.*

FIND IT OUT

case study

Devon's attractions

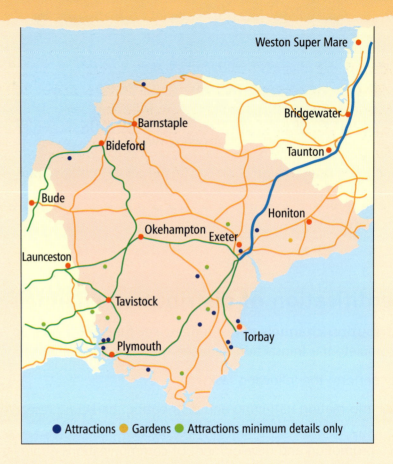

- ● Attractions
- ● Gardens
- ● Attractions minimum details only

These are the major attractions in the county of Devon:

Barbican Glassworks; Babbacombe Model Village; Crownhill Fort; Becky Falls; Coombe Martin Wildlife and Dinosaur Park; Bicton Park Botanical Gardens; Dartmoor Wildlife Park; Buckfast Abbey; Dingles Steam Village; Canonteign Falls; The John Southern Gallery; Ardew Teapottery; The Milkyway Adventure Park; Crealey Park; Morwellham Quay; Hedgehog Hospital; National Marine Aquarium; Otters and Butterflies; Plymouth Dome and Smeaton's Tower; Paignton Zoo; Plymouth Ski Centre; Quad World; The National Shire Horse Centre; Quaywest Waterpark; The Tamar Valley Donkey Park; South Devon Railway; Sorley Tunnel.

Source: Adapted from www.devon-connect.co.uk

Q1 *Draw a map of Devon or visit the www.devon-connect.co.uk website and print out a map of the county.*

Q2 *On the map, mark all of the attractions in the list. You might have to number the attractions and create a key for them.*

Q3 *Identify the main areas of tourism facilities in the county. Where is the greatest concentration of facilities in Devon? Suggest three reasons why they are located there.*

Q4 *Suggest three locations suitable for a day trip for a family. Suggest where the family could spend the night in a hotel or a bed and breakfast by identifying a local village, town or city.*

Promotion

You will have to produce some promotional material for a leisure and tourism organisation for your assessment portfolio in this unit.

Promotion covers all of the ways in which a leisure and tourism organisation tells customers about what it has to sell. The choices of the ways in which the customers are informed differ from product to product but, in most cases, the importance of different forms of promotion is usually in the following order (in terms of the money spent on different promotions, with most important first):

- advertising – paying for advertisements on TV or on the radio or for space in a newspaper or magazine;
- sales promotion – offering deals and discounts or perhaps competitions to attract customers;
- personal selling – training staff to be more effective in making sales to people who approach the business for information and help;
- public relations – sponsoring local events, football clubs or teams and making sure that good news stories about the business appear in newspapers, on TV and on the radio.

We will look at each of these different types of promotion in more detail later, but let's first look at what is behind promotions. The type of promotion used will depend on what the business wants to do and how it normally sells its products or services:

- *Push or pull*. There are two ways of selling, known as **push strategies** or **pull strategies**. A push strategy means that the business spends most of its effort making other businesses do the selling for them. Pull strategies concentrate on making customers interested in the product or service so that they go out to buy it.
- *Buyer readiness*. How ready are the customers to buy the product or the service? Promotion begins with the business telling customers that it exists, then trying to convince them that they want the product. Once this has been achieved, the customers should be convinced enough to go out and buy. This means that advertising and public relations play the major role during this stage. Liking, preference and conviction are more affected by personal selling. Closing the sale is mostly done with sales calls and sales promotions.
- *Product life cycle stage*. In the introduction stage, advertising and public relations are good for producing high awareness, and sales promotion is useful in promoting trial purchases. During growth, advertising and public relations are still very important. In maturity, sales promotion becomes important again because buyers know the brands, and promotion can aid or prevent **brand switching**. In decline, advertising is used to remind people of the product, and public relations are

THE JARGON DRAGON

push strategy – the business promotes the product or service to other businesses that sell the products or services direct to the customer; because the business offers a good deal to retailers, the retailer will make more effort to sell their products – this is known as 'pushing' through the distribution channel

pull strategy – means that the business spends most of its money on advertising and promotion to build up customer demand; if the strategy is successful, consumers will ask retailers for the product, retailers will ask wholesalers, and wholesalers will buy from the business – this is called 'pulling' the product through the distribution channel

brand switching – when customers decide that they want to try another product (an example could be a person who usually likes McDonald's deciding to eat at Burger King or Pizza Hut instead)

dropped. Sales promotion, however, might be strong, as the business seeks to squeeze every last penny from the product.

Any form of promotion relies on the business being able to get its message across to the customer. This means that what it says and how it says it, along with the promotion method it chooses, has to be right. The communication process is complicated and can be interrupted.

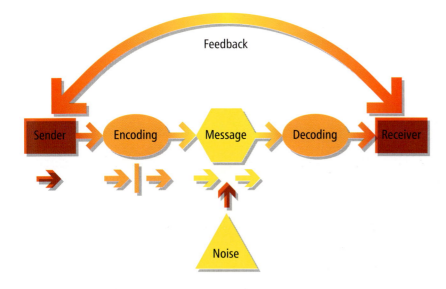

- Sender – the business that wishes to send a message across to the customer.
- Encoding – the way the message is constructed in the form of words and images.
- Message – the actual advertisement that is sent.
- Media – the communication or promotion method used to get the message from the sender to the receiver, for example television, newspapers, magazines, billboards or the Internet.
- Decoding – what the receivers make of the message, how they understand the message.
- Receiver – the customer or target market at which the message is aimed.
- Feedback – how the customer or target market replies to the message. Do they go out and buy the product or service or contact the business for more information?
- Noise – all of the other promotions and communications that are going on at the same time, such as other businesses promoting their products and services.

Remember that we see and hear hundreds of these messages every day. The trick is to make your message stand out.

Think
IT THROUGH

Can you think of at least four recent advertisements or promotions that you have seen recently? What are they and what is it that you remember about them? Why do you think they are easy to remember?

FIND IT OUT

(www.yoke.city.yokohama.jp/articles/00.08 /kusama09.html and www.artoftravel.com)

The first advertisement dates back to 1868 and promotes a hotel in Yokohama, Japan and the second is a modern advertisement for a back-packers' hostel in Sydney, Australia.

Take a visit to the local library and look at the local newspaper archives and find examples of advertisements for local hotels, restaurants or events 25 years ago, 50 years ago and 100 years ago. Try to find advertisements for the same place and see just how much the advertisement and the messages have changed over the years.

Promotional techniques

As we have begun to see, there are several different ways in which businesses try to persuade us to buy or use their products and services. We will now have a look at these different types of promotion in a little more detail.

Advertisements

Advertising is any paid form of presentation and promotion of ideas, goods or services by a business. Advertisements include *print* (magazines, newspapers, direct mail), *broadcast* (television, radio) and *display* (billboards, signs, posters).

Local, national and international leisure and tourism businesses use advertisements. Local newspapers may contain advertisements from businesses not only in the immediate area, but also from national or international companies. National newspapers are very effective advertising media for a variety of different businesses. Nationally distributed magazines are also widely used and they have the advantage of offering colour advertisements.

Television can be too expensive for many leisure and tourism businesses, but the larger attractions and tour operators often use TV to attract customers or to encourage them to call their booking lines.

Radio is cheaper, offering a better breakdown of the type of listeners, so leisure and tourism businesses can more precisely target their advertising.

Display advertising, particularly poster sites and sites at railway stations or bus stops, can be effective, particularly if there are considerable numbers of people or vehicles passing the site.

Direct marketing

Direct marketing attempts to cut out intermediaries and the need to spend vast amounts of money on advertising and other promotions. In effect, direct marketing is direct selling – in other words the business contacts customers directly and attempts to persuade them to buy.

Direct marketing aims to obtain an immediate buying response. Major forms of direct marketing include:

- Direct mail and catalogue marketing (used by many tour operators)
- Telemarketing or phone selling (less common in the industry, but used by some leisure clubs to recruit members)
- Television marketing, including **infomercials** and shopping networks (these are being increasingly used by the travel and tourism industry and can be seen on Sky Travel, Travel Channel and Travel Channel 2 on satellite television)
- Online shopping (in addition to tour operators or major attractions having their own websites, flights and packages are available via other general websites, such as Kelkoo and Opodo).

THE JARGON DRAGON

Infomercial – an advertisement that has plenty of information for the customer but is designed to make the customer want to buy after being given all the details

FIND IT OUT

How do businesses that use direct marketing obtain the names, addresses and telephone numbers of potential customers so that they can contact them?

Successful direct marketing begins with a good database, which can be used to locate potential customers, tailor goods and services, and target marketing communications.

Public relations

Public relations is intended to build good relations with the business's customers by obtaining favourable publicity, building up a good corporate image, and handling or heading off unfavourable rumours, stories and events.

Public relations activities involve creating news stories, features and events that seem more real to readers than advertisements. Public relations can also reach many customers who avoid salespeople and advertisements. The message gets to the buyer as 'news' rather than as a sales effort. Like advertising, public relations can make a business and its products or services seem exciting.

Personal selling

Personal selling is a two-way communication aimed at making sales and building customer relationships. A good salesperson listens to the customer and reacts to the information they are being told. Product-related information can be tailored to the individual (or group) and presented in a way that is meaningful and understandable to the customer.

Personal selling tools include sales presentations, trade shows, and **incentive programmes**. Exhibitions, such as The Travel Show, offer tour operators an excellent opportunity to meet customers face-to-face and use sales people with specialised skills. Travel agents use sales techniques to convince customers to book with them and not a rival business. Other leisure and tourism businesses use telephone sales advisors to respond to customer enquiries.

THE JARGON DRAGON

incentive programmes – paying salespeople a bonus or a percentage of every sale that they make

Displays

Displays in travel agents or at visitor attractions and public places such as libraries can be quite effective in creating interest

and sales. The business needs to create a display that is attractive and will encourage the customers to look. Displays often have leaflets for the customers to take away with them, or salespeople there to try to make personal sales while the customer is still interested in the product or service that is being displayed.

Displays are also often seen at major leisure, travel or tourism exhibitions. This is an ideal place to promote products and services as every person who visits the show is interested in the kind of products and services on offer.

Using the Internet, find out the names, dates and locations of at least three leisure, travel or tourism shows or events in the United Kingdom this year.

Sponsorship

Sponsorship is a business relationship between a provider of funds, resources or services and an individual, event or organisation that offers in return some rights and association that may be used for commercial advantage.

The Institute of Sports Sponsorship

The Institute of Sports Sponsorship was founded in 1985 with Prince Philip as its President, to be the representative voice of the sports sponsorship industry. The ISS promotes best practice in sponsorship, works closely with sports bodies, government and the media to improve understanding; and lobbies on behalf of its membership on key issues.

Bringing sport and business together, the ISS gives commercial interests the opportunity to network and influence, adding value to the basic sponsorship contract.

Members of the ISS include many of the major sponsoring companies in the United Kingdom as well as consultancies, research agencies, sports law practices and so forth. As well as representing the industry's interests regarding national and international sponsorship, the ISS has promoted the development of sports sponsorship at grass roots and, since 1992, has administered, in England, the government's business sponsorship incentive scheme for grass roots sport, Sportsmatch.

Source: www.sports-sponsorship.co.uk

Q1 *Visit the* www.sports-sponsorship.co.uk *website and find out how much money is being spent on sports sponsorship each year.*

Q2 *Briefly note what a sponsor would get from the relationship with the organisation, event or individual it sponsors (for example a business that has its name on the front of a football shirt).*

Q3 *What is the purpose of the Institute's code of conduct?*

Q4 *What do you understand by the term 'government's business sponsorship incentive scheme for grass roots sport'?*

Demonstrations

Showing potential customers what it would be like to be able to use a service or the benefits of buying a product is difficult in most cases for the leisure and tourism industry. How could an airline show what it would be like on one of its flights, or how could Alton Towers let potential customers feel the thrill of its latest ride?

Many sports centres, health and fitness clubs and other organisations can put on successful demonstrations to show what it is like to take part in the kinds of activities and sports on offer. The problem is, where does the demonstration take place and how much room would be needed? Many of these demonstrations would take place at events where it would be possible to show just how exciting and beneficial the sport or the activity would be.

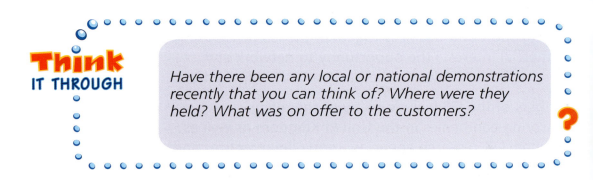

Think IT THROUGH

Have there been any local or national demonstrations recently that you can think of? Where were they held? What was on offer to the customers?

Sales promotions

Sales promotion is the use of short-term incentives to encourage the purchase or sale of a product or service. The key term is 'short term', as most sales promotions only last for a matter of weeks or months or, in some cases, days.

Sales promotions aimed at the consumer are often at the 'point of sale' (for example, in-store displays or on packages) and have a 'buy me NOW!' message. Other sales promotion tools include discounts, coupons and 'free' goods.

Although this is also a non-personal form of communication, many sales promotion themes are intended to spark personal interest in the product or service being promoted.

> Collect some examples of sales promotion leaflets, such as money-off vouchers or discount coupons. How are they communicating to the customer? What incentive to buy are they giving the customer?

Promotional materials

Now that we have looked at some of the main methods of promoting products and services, let's turn our attention to what the customer actually sees: the promotional materials themselves.

It is important to realise that advertisers cannot just say what they please about the product or the service, there are rules to make sure that the advertisers do not mislead customers. The British Codes of Advertising and Sales Promotion contain a number of requirements for holiday and travel advertisements. As a general rule, no advertisement should mislead consumers about anything likely to influence their decision about buying a holiday. The rules require advertisers to make sure that:

- all prices should be inclusive of all taxes or charges paid for at the point of purchase of the ticket – any extras such as insurance, booking fee or surcharges should be stated;
- any limitations must be clear – if, for example, a price is dependent on two people travelling together and sharing a room this should be specified;
- the date of travel must also be clear;
- itineraries must be accurate both in terms of places visited and the amount of time spent there;
- all amenities that are advertised (such as golf courses, shops, child care) should be available – if they cannot be used during the off-peak season this should be made clear;
- if illustrations and photographs are used they must be up to date and accurate – the brochure should also make every effort not to omit any significant drawbacks regarding the location of accommodation, such as nearby building works, busy roads or airports.

Visit the Advertising Standards Authority website
(www.asa.org.uk) and find out more about the
rules governing advertisers.

Design, words and images

Leisure and tourism organisations, just like any other business, will attempt to design their advertisements and other promotional materials to achieve the greatest impact on their potential customers. A customer not only has to be attracted to the material, but has to retain interest for long enough for the message the business wishes to get across to have the desired effect on the customer. This means that the material, in whatever form, has to have an ideal balance of words and images, in the most appropriate design for the intended audience. The main points of the material need to be obvious (usually larger print, or a different colour or font) and attractive and eye-catching photographs or other images used to attract and keep the attention. Above all, whatever the material seeks to prompt the customer to do, such as call a telephone number, send in a coupon or visit a website, it must be clear, obvious and offer a solution to whatever the customer might require.

Advertisements

Advertisements, as we have seen, cover paid-for space on television or radio or in newspapers and magazines. They also include poster sites (such as boards beside roads, at airports and at sports venues). It is important to try to place the advertisements not only in places where the maximum number of people will see them but also in places where the ideal target markets are likely to see and respond to them.

Brochures and leaflets

Brochures, in particular, are extremely important in the leisure and tourism industry. Brochures are one of the main methods by which tour operators sell their holiday packages. Customers need to know a great deal about a holiday, including the resort and the hotel details, as they are preparing to spend a considerable amount of money with the operator.

case study

New Hampshire – tourism advertisements

Advertisements ('ads') for New Hampshire Tourism feature scenic beauty with messages that communicate an authentic experience. These ads have produced a rate of return of $9 for every $1 spent on promotion. In addition, in a recent conversion study, 65% of those surveyed were influenced to visit New Hampshire by promotional materials.

Source: Adapted from www.bywinc.com.

Q1 *What do you understand by the term 'rate of return'?*

Q2 *If New Hampshire spent $1 000 000 on advertising, how much would it expect the state to receive from tourist income?*

case study

2003 Tourism brochures and initiatives unveiled

North Norfolk District Council has published its tourism brochures for the year 2003, coinciding with the launch of two new initiatives designed to better support the local tourism industry.

Ninety-five thousand copies of the *Coast, Countryside and Boating Holidays* accommodation brochure have been printed (5000 more than last year), along with 300 000 copies of the *So Much to See and Do* attractions guide.

A campaign of advertising these brochures in the national media has already begun, starting with the Christmas edition of the *Radio Times*.

Source: www.northnorfolk.org.

Q1 *Which local tourism businesses are supported by the council in the* Coast, Countryside and Boating Holidays *brochure?*

Q2 *Find out how many copies of the* Radio Times *are sold each week. You could find this information from the British Rate and Data (BRAD), which should be in your school library or local reference library.*

Q3 *If each of the brochures cost the council 56p to print, what was the total bill for all of the brochures?*

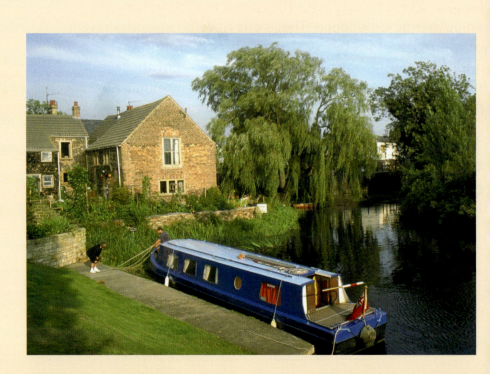

Merchandising materials

Merchandising materials are items that have the name and logo of a leisure and tourism business on them. Typical examples are mugs, car stickers, badges and other items such as calendars. Some of the items are given away to encourage customers to display them in their cars or so that other people can see the name and logo and perhaps be interested in visiting the site.

Other tourist attractions offer merchandising materials for sale to help raise extra money. Examples would be museums and zoos, which offer a wide range of items from mousemats to writing pads and even books and videos with their names and logos for sale on-site, by mail order, or over the Internet.

Videos

Videos can be useful in showing customers what it might be like to visit a tourist attraction (several larger attractions use videos such as Disneyland Paris), but it is now far more effective to use short video clips on websites where the customer can instantly see the attraction or destination, and the business or tourist information organisation does not have to cover the costs of sending out videos.

Press releases

Press releases are designed to obtain free space in the media for news stories about the business or organisation. The most important consideration is to make the news story interesting enough for the media to bother to run it. The main things that the media will be looking for are a 'human interest angle' (which means that they can help relate the story to their readers, viewers or listeners and that there is a quotation or two from someone to give the story a bit of life). The story has to be some kind of genuine news such as a major development, a new initiative, a new ride, an award won by the organisation or something similar.

Internet sites

Websites are not just a useful way of selling to customers – they are also an excellent way to give customers a great deal of information and keep them up to date. They can be used to show the attraction, event or other facility extremely well with numerous photographs, maps and drawings as well as contact names, addresses, telephone numbers and email addresses.

Internet sites are also useful to help link up a series of different leisure facilities or attractions in a particular area. Each website of the group can carry advertisements and links to the other members of the group so that they can all benefit from the support of the other members.

SWOT analysis

SWOT analysis is a very useful technique for looking at the overall future of a leisure and tourism organisation. SWOT analysis covers the following aspects, the first two considerations look at the internal workings of the organisation.

- *Strengths* – what is the organisation or business good at? What are its key advantages over the competition in terms of its products and services as well as its facilities, customer service and expertise of employees?
- *Weaknesses* – what is the organisation not good at? Where does the business fall down in terms of the ways it does things? Are the products and services good enough? Are the building, the facilities or the attractions of poor quality? Are the staff not very good at handling customers?
- *Opportunities* – what is happening *outside* the organisation that offers opportunities? Has the transport system in the area been improved? Has a major competitor closed down? Is the area more popular than in the past? Is the local council spending money on promoting the area?
- *Threats* – what is happening *outside* the organisation that could threaten it? Are there more competitors? Are there problems with the area? Perhaps a nearby area has received investment, which might mean that the local area is now less attractive for the business.

The diagram on the left is a common SWOT analysis grid that helps to place all of the considerations in the right position.

It may be useful to look at the business from a wider view; the diagram at the top of the next page helps to place the business in the world in which it operates.

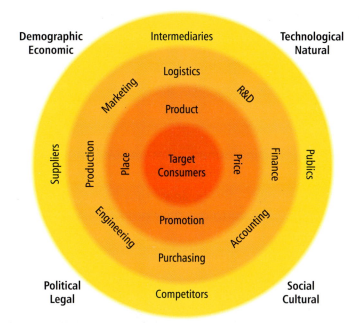

The business, as we have seen, tries to target the right type of customers to buy their products or services, but there are many other influences out there that can affect the chances that businesses have of being successful in doing this.

Taking the target customers as being central to the business, they try to attract them by using the 'four Ps'. This effort is supported by the departments of the business, which may include:

- marketing – which uses the marketing mix;
- logistics – which brings the products or services to the customer;
- research and development – which comes up with new ideas to sell to the customers;
- accounts and finance – which control and monitor the income and costs and work out whether the business is making a profit;
- purchasing – which buys products and services to sell on to the customer;

How would the departments of a leisure and tourism business differ if one business sold tangible products and the other sold services?

FIND IT OUT

- engineering – which considers how products can be made;
- production – which organises the making of products to sell to the customers.

Outside the organisation, there are at least four other factors that will affect whether a business can or cannot do what it wants. These are:

- suppliers – the business relies on suppliers to be able to sell it the products and services that it needs;
- intermediaries – the business may rely on intermediaries, as we have seen, to get their products and services to the customers;
- publics – these are groups outside the business that have an interest in what the business is doing, such as the local council, the tourist board or government;
- competitors – these can have a huge impact on what the business does. Competitors may launch a big advertising campaign to take customers away, they may drop their prices or they may start offering products and services that the business wanted to move into at a later date.

FIND IT OUT

Suggest five other outside groups or publics that would be interested in a local swimming pool.

Beyond these are four other important areas that can affect the business. These are:

- Demographic and economic – changes in population, number of teenagers and how much people are earning and have to spend.
- Political and legal – what laws might affect the way the business is run? Are there new health and safety rules?
- Technological and natural – what new products and services have been designed? Do they offer the business more opportunities? Natural changes, such as more rain, may make a theme park less likely to be able to open on days when there is poor weather. This might mean that it is not a good idea to site an attraction in an area that does not have good weather.
- Social and cultural – are there any changes in what people prefer to do? Are there new trends and fashions that might affect the business?

Can you think of two different leisure activities that have become popular in recent years? Are there facilities for them? Can you think of two that are no longer very popular? What has happened to the facilities that used to cater for these?

FIND IT OUT

Now let's look at a practical example of SWOT analysis. Here are the key parts of Maidstone Borough Council's own tourism SWOT analysis (a full version can be found at www.digitalmaidstone.co.uk).

Strengths	Weaknesses
Easy access from London	Bypassed by travellers
Easy access from ports	No major town-centre attraction
Large local population	Traffic in town-centre
Good retail centre	No large town-centre hotel
Good hotels	Not many town-centre smaller
Not seasonal	hotels and bed and breakfast
Good public transport	Ugly modern buildings
Theatre, museums and night clubs	Poor range of restaurants
Leeds Castle	Town centre is dirty
Museum of Kent Rural Life	Confusing signposting
Good local bed-and-breakfast	Lack of historic interest
Good range of sports, attractions and other facilitiesi	Expensive for foreign visitors

Opportunities	Threats
New itineraries for different target markets	Downturn in visitor numbers
Kent is known by overseas visitors	Rise in prices of cross-channel ferries
Advertising evening shopping and events	High-speed rail link to London cuts out Maidstone as a stop
New Carriage Museum	Other regional centres have better reputation
New retail park	Increased traffic congestion
New website	Poor central government support
New promotion for town parks and open spaces	
Partnership with Kent Tourism	
Changes in traffic flows	
Upgrade old parts of town	

FIND IT OUT

Think of four strengths, weakness, opportunities and threats for your own local area.

Promotional campaigns

A promotional campaign is best described as a series of related promotional activities which are designed to have an overall impact. In other words, the different promotional activities would seek to support one another and reinforce the message to the audience they have been designed to reach. A campaign may involve the business placing advertisements in newspapers or magazines over a period of time, supported by posters or radio advertising, briefly repeating what the printed advertisements include.

Campaigns usually run for a definite period of time, perhaps in the lead up to the launching of a tour operator's brochure, or to promote last-minute deals. Other campaigns can be run in order to remind customers of an ongoing service offered by the business and to generally increase their awareness of the business's products or services. Each campaign will have a definite goal and the business will hope that its chosen mix of promotional methods will achieve the main purpose.

The best way to look at how a promotional campaign would work is to examine what happened in a real campaign. This section of the unit looks at what happened with a campaign run by Disneyland Paris.

Objectives of a promotional campaign

In October 1999, Disneyland Paris was featuring a new themed area transforming 'Frontierland' into 'Halloweenland', and wanted to actively promote this 'limited edition' attraction leading up to and during the whole month of October whilst at the same time reinforcing the 'fun' and 'friendly' values of the theme park.

Radio was an ideal medium to reach listeners every day, and particularly young families, in the build up to Halloween. It also provided the right environment for portraying the fun and light-hearted brand values of Disneyland.

Heart 106.2 was chosen to reach family audiences in London. Presenters across all shows encouraged young listeners to write and send in scary stories under the title of 'My Halloween Adventure'. During the first three weeks in October, a different story was picked out each day and broadcast on the 'Jono and the Morning Crew' breakfast show. Some selected stories were also given a special 'Halloween recording' with Vincent Price and special sound effects.

The 15 winning entries over the three-week period won a trip for their families to Disneyland Paris at the end of October. Overall the campaign reached an estimated 1.6 million listeners in London.

The station received over 1500 entries. The eerie tone of the winning stories, which were read out on air right in the middle of the breakfast show, made them stand out. Furthermore, station enthusiasm for the event meant that it received a lot of enthusiastic talk-up from DJs for both Disneyland Paris and their partners, Eurostar, throughout the month of October.

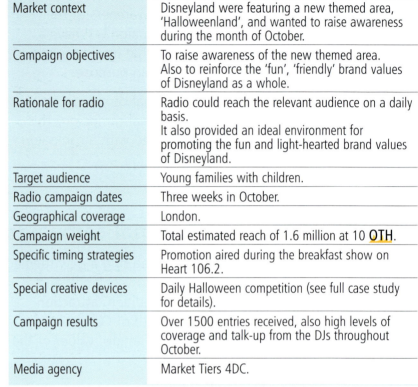

Company	Disneyland Paris
Market context	Disneyland were featuring a new themed area, 'Halloweenland', and wanted to raise awareness during the month of October.
Campaign objectives	To raise awareness of the new themed area. Also to reinforce the 'fun', 'friendly' brand values of Disneyland as a whole.
Rationale for radio	Radio could reach the relevant audience on a daily basis. It also provided an ideal environment for promoting the fun and light-hearted brand values of Disneyland.
Target audience	Young families with children.
Radio campaign dates	Three weeks in October.
Geographical coverage	London.
Campaign weight	Total estimated reach of 1.6 million at 10 **OTH**.
Specific timing strategies	Promotion aired during the breakfast show on Heart 106.2.
Special creative devices	Daily Halloween competition (see full case study for details).
Campaign results	Over 1500 entries received, also high levels of coverage and talk-up from the DJs throughout October.
Media agency	Market Tiers 4DC.

Source: Radio Advertising Bureau www.rab.co.uk

THE JARGON DRAGON

OTH – opportunities to hear – the number of times that an average listener could hear the promotion on the radio station

Portfolio building

You will need to study two organisations, one of which you will have to choose to look at in detail. You must produce a portfolio based on your investigations into the marketing activities of a leisure or a tourism organisation and compare it to another organisation. You will have to include the following in your portfolio:

- A description of the four Ps of your organisation and how they help the business achieve its objectives;
- Collect a piece of promotional material designed to attract a particular audience;

- An assessment of the techniques and materials used by your organisation, as well as the market research methods used to identify target markets;
- A comparison of your organisation's promotional campaigns with the promotional campaign of a second organisation.

Customer Service

What's in this unit?

All leisure and tourism organisations depend on their customers. They cannot succeed without them. Customer service is, therefore, one of the most important things an organisation can provide to keep the customers it has and attract new ones.

In this unit you will:

- discover why customer service is so important and learn about the different needs of customers;
- understand how organisations try to meet these needs;
- learn about personal presentation and how important it is when dealing with customers;
- see how organisations deal with dissatisfied customers and learn how you could deal with them yourself;
- understand why it is important for organisations to keep customer records.

This unit is internally assessed. You will have to:

- look at the benefits to an organisation, its employees and its customers of providing a good level of customer service;
- produce a portfolio of evidence that shows you have reviewed the customer service provided by a leisure or tourism organisation;
- prove that you can describe situations in which staff deal with customers;
- prove that you can describe the type of customer records that the organisation keeps;
- prove that you have looked at how the organisation meets the needs of its customers, how it communicates with them, and how it deals with any complaints they have made.

In this unit you will learn about:

What is customer service?

THE JARGON DRAGON

needs – essential products and services required by customers, such as food and clothes

wants – products or services that are not essential but are desired by customers, such as luxuries like holidays

A business is unable to survive without customers. However large or small a business may be, it will always want to make sure that its customers are happy. The customers' **needs**, **wants** and requirements change all the time, so the business will have to think ahead of its customers to make sure it always gives them exactly what they require to make them satisfied.

Customer satisfaction is achieved when the service given to customers meets their needs. Obviously, those customers who leave a leisure and tourism facility feeling satisfied with the service they have received are more likely to return.

Happy customers may also tell their friends about the good service and the facility will become more popular.

Think IT THROUGH

Why do you think it is important to an organisation that its customers return? Discuss this as a group.

?

Different types of leisure and tourism facility will provide different types of service to their customers. A hotel, for example, will provide a different range of services from a swimming pool or a sports venue. However, each will have many different types of customer and all of them could have different needs.

Before we look at customer service in more detail, think about your local swimming pool. Write a list of the different types of people that you have seen using this facility. Are they all of the same age group? Are they all good at swimming?

The most important reasons for providing a good customer service are:

- if customers are treated well they will return to the organisation;
- if customers have received good service from the organisation, they will tell their family and friends;
- if customers tell their friends and family about a good organisation, then this will mean that the organisation will have a good image.

To achieve a good level of customer service a leisure and tourism facility would have to think about the following main issues:

- Meeting the needs of its different types of customers – this can be difficult if customers have a huge range of different needs. The business will try to make sure that the bulk of its customers are happy and that they receive a level of service that is acceptable.
- Making sure that the leisure and tourism facility is healthy, safe and secure for the customers. Health and safety is an important issue in a leisure and tourism facility, both for the customers and for the people working there.

If possible visit your local swimming pool and answer the following questions:

1. Does the swimming pool offer its customers a secure place to keep their belongings while they are swimming?
2. Is there a lifeguard on duty at all times?
3. Are there notices placed around the pool to tell customers about what is dangerous?
4. What other health, safety and security services does the swimming pool offer its customers?

If effective customer service is to be achieved then the organisation will have to plan properly. It would have to do this:

- to make sure it has enough trained staff;
- to make sure it has enough equipment and the money to have it maintained regularly;
- to make sure that the facility itself is designed well.

Let's think about the design of the facility first, as customers will expect the design to be pleasing to the eye and attractive.

The customer needs to feel comfortable in all areas of the facility and the organisation can help to make this so by:

- providing plenty of parking space outside the facility;
- making sure the main reception area is obvious as customers walk in the door;
- making sure there is always someone at the reception desk so that new customers can ask for help;
- making sure that places like changing rooms and toilets are easy to find by providing direction notices;
- providing suitable facilities for disabled people, for example, toilets, ramps to get into the building and car parking spaces;
- providing the correct type of lighting, for example bright lights for activity areas and softer lighting for relaxation areas;
- making sure the customers can see that the facility is health, safety and security aware by providing fire

extinguishers, doors, alarms and exits. There should also be a first aid room and health and safety notices.

It is also important that the staff of the organisation are clear about what to do in the case of an emergency of some kind.

FIND IT OUT

All businesses that have employees, customers and visitors have to make sure they provide a healthy and safe environment. Have a look at www.hse.gov.uk. *This is the website of the Health and Safety Executive (HSE), which tries to make sure that businesses comply with health and safety laws. Click on 'L' in the alphabet at the top of their home page and this will take you to the leisure section.*

How many leaflets does the HSE provide for the different parts of the leisure industry?

Having enough staff is just one part of the problem. There is no point in having a lot of staff available to deal with customers if these employees are not well trained. The staff in a leisure and tourism business would have to have certain skills and experience in dealing with customers. The experience only comes with time. New or young and inexperienced employees can learn a lot from people who have worked for the organisation for a longer period of time.

Training basically falls into four different categories. These are:

- On-the-job training – training that is carried out while at work. Often someone who has been in the job for a long

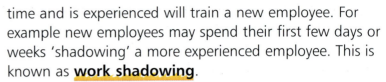

work shadowing – new employees spending their first few days or weeks with a more experienced employee to learn the job

time and is experienced will train a new employee. For example new employees may spend their first few days or weeks 'shadowing' a more experienced employee. This is known as **work shadowing**.

- Off-the-job training – training is carried out at somewhere other than the workplace, for example in a college of further education or a training agency.
- Part-time training – the employee could attend a school, college or training agency for day release, evening classes or a short course.
- Full-time training – the employee is taken out of the workplace for a period of time, sometimes to attend a short course but often to attend a course that could last a year or longer.

Obtain a copy of your local college's prospectus. This is like a catalogue that shows you all the courses that the college runs. For each course in the prospectus, write beside it the categories given above to which it relates.

When we think about training we also need to identify two main types of qualification that you could achieve.

- *Vocational training or qualifications* are those that are directly related to the job being done. It does not always matter whether you are in work or not, as you practise doing the different tasks involved in the job. National Vocational Qualifications (NVQs) are available in the leisure and tourism industry. They include qualifications at Levels 1 to 4 in subjects such as customer service, administration and travel services or sport and recreation.
- *Non-vocational training or qualifications* are those that may not have a direct link with a particular job but are more general. Often these are called academic qualifications.

The leisure and tourism organisation will also have set procedures for dealing with customers. Employees have to be made aware of these when they first start their jobs. Sometimes organisations issue booklets to all of the employees and these contain the procedures for dealing with customers.

The procedures will apply to all aspects of customer care. This might include, for example, the different ways customers should be led from the organisation's buildings in the case of an emergency of some kind. Emergencies include:

- fire;
- chemical leakage;
- bomb alerts;
- violence or threats by a member of the public;
- children losing their parents or guardians.

> *Your school must have procedures in place for evacuation in case of fire or bomb alerts. Find out what these procedures are if you don't already know.*

FIND IT OUT

If all the employees are working with a good knowledge of these procedures then they will all be doing the same thing. This will help to make sure that members of staff are treating the customers in the same way. It will help the organisation to give its existing and potential customers a more professional and efficient image of their facility. If a business is to provide an efficient and effective customer service then trained and experienced staff will have to carry out a variety of different tasks to a high standard.

Customer service is all about **effectiveness**, **efficiency** and **reliability**. Often an organisation will make a commitment to its customers by producing a charter. This makes promises about the standard of service a customer can expect from the organisation.

THE JARGON DRAGON

effectiveness – achieving something that one sets out to do

efficiency – working with the least waste of effort; being competent

reliability – able to be trusted and dependable

case study

A customer charter

Look at the example of a tour operator's customer charter given below, then answer the questions at the end.

Price guarantee
Should a hotel, or any other operator, offer a like-for-like package, cheaper to you directly, we will refund the difference!

Customer satisfaction
In the unlikely event that you experience a problem and have cause to make a written complaint, we will respond within 14 days of receipt. If we fail to do this you will be entitled to a £10 voucher to use as part-payment of another trip.

Service
We are at your service seven days a week, via the Internet.

Meeting your every need
Should your first choice of break not be available, we promise to offer you an appropriate alternative. Don't forget that you can make your reservation right up until the last minute – even on your chosen date of travel.

Ticket despatch
All tickets and travel documents will be despatched to you the same day for bookings made before 13:00 or, for bookings made after 13:00, the next working day.

Peace of mind
Your room will still be secured in the event of your late arrival at a hotel.

Q1 *Why do you think a travel and tourism organisation would want to offer a charter to its customers?*

Q2 *What are the benefits to the business of producing such a charter?*

Q3 *What are the benefits to the customer of receiving such a charter?*

Anyone helping an organisation to provide a good customer service would carry out the following jobs on a regular basis.

Providing information and advice to customers

Customers need a range of information to help them use the facility. They will expect the staff at the facility to give them all the information they need. For this reason it is very important that the staff have the following **skills**:

- they can understand what is being asked;
- they can provide the information being requested;
- they understand how important it is, both for the customer and for the organisation, that the question is answered properly.

Customers often expect all employees of an organisation to be experts. They ask a variety of different questions about, for example, how to use the facilities or how to use a specific piece of equipment. Staff need to be trained to give professional and clear advice when required.

The advice a customer might require includes:

- Information about the different **products** or **services** that the facility might offer. They should make sure they are clear about what the customer wants. It may be that they need information or advice about the price of the product or it could be that they have to sell the product to them. If this is the case, then they will have been trained by the organisation to cope with the different ways customers can pay for products and services:

THE JARGON DRAGON

skills – abilities of employees which help them carry out their work

THE JARGON DRAGON

product – a general term used to describe goods or services offered by a business

service – a general term used to describe everything other than products that may be sold by a business

- cheques;
- cash;
- debit cards;
- credit cards.

THE JARGON DRAGON

coaching – showing the participants of a sport or activity what to do; coaching is also a training method to show employees how to make sure customers receive a good level of service from the organisation

- Information about **coaching** sessions at the leisure facility or about the outdoor activities they run. When staff are coaching for a sport or activity, such as dancing classes, it is expected that they will know what they are doing – but it is the same if they are just giving information about the coaching sessions. To the customer they will be regarded as experts who know exactly what to do and when to do it.

Before anyone could start a coaching class, the facility would need to find out:

- if they have ever participated in the sport or activity before;
- if they have had any training before;
- how old they are;
- how many people were interested in the coaching – it might be that there is a set number that need to be involved before the session can go ahead;
- the days and times the sessions are due to be run;
- the cost of each session.

Why is it important for a facility to obtain the information listed above before someone begins a coaching class? For each of the items we have listed give your reasons why you consider it to be important.

Visit the Alton Towers' website at www.alton-towers.co.uk. Choose the INFO option at the top of their home page. What information do they provide to their customers? Answer the following questions:

1. *What information do they provide to the customer about getting to the park?*
2. *What information do they provide to the customer about where to stay near to the park?*
3. *What information do they provide to the customer about their opening times?*

Now visit Chessington World of Adventures website at www.chessington.co.uk and answer the same questions about this theme park.

Receiving and passing on messages

Everyone working for an organisation would be expected to take messages for people who are not available from time to time. If this is the case then there will probably be an organisational procedure for the way the caller is greeted. There may also be a message form that all employees would use to write the message on. This is particularly important in the case of a telephone message as there is often more information to remember. A typical telephone message form would include the following headings:

- the caller's name;
- the caller's company or personal address;
- the caller's company or personal telephone number;
- the message that has to be passed on;
- any particular action the caller needs the organisation to take.

Name _Charles Farley_

Address _22 Letsbe Avenue, Anytown_

Phone No. _01055 987654_

Message _Caller is having trouble installing software onto computer – where is software going?_

Action _Can you ring a.s.a.p?_

There are some key points to remember when taking a message for someone else. These are:

- listen carefully to what the person is saying;
- if you don't understand what the other person is saying, ask him or her to repeat it;
- always say the message and details of telephone numbers and names back to the caller so they can hear that you have understood it correctly;
- promise the caller you will pass the message on – *and make sure that you do!*

Keeping records

Keeping accurate and up-to-date records of customers who use a facility is another vital part of customer service.

Whilst individual records of customers may not be appropriate for many tourist attractions, record keeping is essential to facilities such as leisure centres, or indeed libraries and other centres which have a regular customer base.

The records, as we will see later in this Unit, tend to be computerised and contain information such as name, address, contact telephone numbers, email addresses, payment details, previous bookings made, advance booking and, in some cases, health details. Many smaller facilities keep these records on simple file cards or on forms kept in individual files, organised alphabetically.

The records are essential as they allow a member of staff to either look up the customer's information or find it in the filing system and have it to hand when they are talking with that customer.

It is essential to ensure that all members of staff know the procedure and the fact that they need to update the records whenever they have cause to have contact with the customer.

Providing assistance

Sometimes customers may need help and assistance. This will often be of a practical nature – for instance, they might require change for a locker or vending machine. At other times wheelchair users or others with a disability of some kind may require assistance to gain access into a particular part of the leisure facility. Whatever the nature of the request, the employees should always be polite and show customers that they are happy to help them. It is important that, however small the request for assistance might be, customers feel that they are valued and that the staff actually care about them.

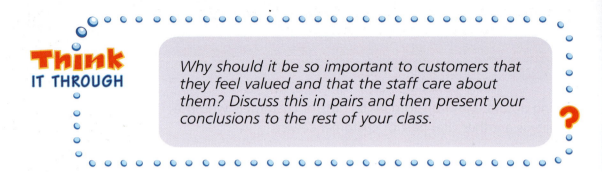

Think IT THROUGH

Why should it be so important to customers that they feel valued and that the staff care about them? Discuss this in pairs and then present your conclusions to the rest of your class.

Dealing with problems and dissatisfied customers

THE JARGON DRAGON

complaints – a customer who feels that the organisation has not acted correctly might complain in writing, by telephone or personally at the organisation itself

More often than not, dealing with problems means dealing with **complaints** from dissatisfied customers.

Staff should always be able to deal with these complaints and respond positively to the customer. They should make sure that they:

- listen carefully to what is being said;
- ask questions to make sure they understand exactly what the complaint is about;
- explain to the customer what they can do to help them with the problem;
- obtain help from someone else if it is a problem they can't deal with themselves;
- keep the customer informed of what is being done at all times.

THE JARGON DRAGON

abusive customers are those who threaten employees or who swear and show the possibility that they could become violent

Sometimes customers become angry. If this happens employees should make sure they remain calm and do not argue back. The old saying goes 'the customer is always right' but this is not always the case. Sometimes customers become angry because they know they are wrong. But this doesn't mean an employee has the right to be rude to a customer, even if the customer does become **abusive**.

Employees dealing with an abusive customer should:

- apologise for the fact that the customer is upset about something to do with the organisation;

- show sympathy – for example, tell the customer they understand why the customer is so upset;
- ask the right questions to get to the bottom of what the customer is complaining about;
- let the customer see they are going to try to do something about the problem;
- get someone to deal with the situation as quickly as possible;
- try to explain to the customer what is being done at every stage;
- try to explain why the problem might have arisen in the first place;
- not put the blame on someone else;
- try to agree with the customer what would be the best course of action;
- promise the customer that they will do all they can to make sure that the solution actually happens;
- keep their promises.

An organisation that is concerned with improving its customer service will carefully check all the complaints they receive. They will want to know how often different customers complain about the same thing. If they find that complaints about the same subject are occurring regularly, then they will attempt to improve the situation. Often they will have a special form that customers have to complete. Reading these forms will help the organisation's managers to decide if the service can be improved or if extra services can be added to help the customer remain satisfied.

Other organisations have **suggestion boxes** in their reception area so that customers can give them ideas about any extra services they think are needed.

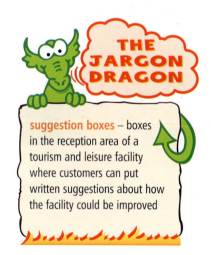

THE JARGON DRAGON

suggestion boxes – boxes in the reception area of a tourism and leisure facility where customers can put written suggestions about how the facility could be improved

Visit three local leisure and tourism facilities. Do any of them have suggestion boxes for their customers to use? If they don't use suggestion boxes, find out what a customer would have to do to make a suggestion about improving customer service in the facility.

FIND IT OUT

Offering extra services

Many leisure and tourism facilities will offer a broader range of services to their customers than simply dealing with their immediate needs. Most customers will require information, assistance or advice. Others will need guidance and careful handling if they are dissatisfied. A leisure and tourism organisation will also try to provide additional services, which, in most circumstances, a customer may not necessarily expect. These types of services aim to reduce the possibility of the customer finding an excuse not to use the facility or visit the attraction. One simple extra service that has many implications is *access*. Ramps, lifts and other easy means of getting from one floor to another are not only essential for those in wheelchairs, but also for families with children in pushchairs, or the elderly, who may find it difficult to climb stairs.

Other extra services could include:

- providing for different dietary needs, such as vegetarians, vegans or those with requirements related to their religion or culture;
- providing rest areas or baby-changing rooms;
- displaying notices in different languages;
- providing personal headphones for those with a visual impairment so that they can hear a commentary about what is being viewed.

Think
IT THROUGH

Choose one leisure or tourism facility that you or someone else in your class has visited. How many extra services does it offer its customers? List them. Why do they add to the customer service the organisation already provides?

Different types of customer

In many leisure and tourism organisations there are different types of customer. It may be easy to cope with some of them but others may need more careful attention. When we talk about customer types, the following list shows what we mean:

- individuals – people who choose to go to their leisure centre or visit an attraction alone;
- groups – this can include couples with children, large groups of children or large groups of adults;
- people of different ages;
- people from different cultures – this means people from different backgrounds or from different countries;
- non-English speakers;
- people with specific needs, for example those who have impaired sight or hearing, those in wheelchairs, or young children;
- business men and women.

By considering each of these different types of customer, an organisation can help to make sure it is providing them all with effective service.

Individuals

For many leisure and tourism organisations the individual is an ideal customer. Single individuals are usually better off than married couples or those with children and have more time and money to spend on their leisure activities. Obviously, individuals make up groups, as we will discover in the next section, but they very often travel to and arrive at their leisure activity alone. More importantly for the organisation, they pay for their leisure activity.

Very often individual customers are of the younger generation and so will be likely to become long-term customers of the leisure and tourism organisation. They could also bring their friends as other individual customers, or, in later years, bring their partner and any children as group customers.

You could be an individual customer. Write a list of all the leisure activities you do. For each activity write what the related leisure facility offers you, as one of its customers. Examples could include private changing rooms, special times when you can use the facility, or any other service that is aimed just at individual customers.

Groups

It is common for families, groups of adults or groups of children to be regular customers of a leisure and tourism facility. Groups tend to be active customers who attend leisure centres and tourist attractions on a regular basis. Because families make up the majority of the population of the United Kingdom, it is fair to say that most of a leisure facility's products, services and activities are popular with groups.

The employees of a leisure and tourism organisation will often find that dealing with groups as customers is very different to dealing with individuals. There is often an individual 'in charge' of the group and most discussions about arrangements would be through that one person.

In cases when an adult is in charge of a group of children, such as on school trips or visits, then the person in charge is obvious. In other cases the employee would need to be sure that there is no confusion about who the group leader may be. Employees would have to make sure that they treat each member of the group in the same way and not simply direct all their conversations through one person.

A club, company or other type of organisation might have an ongoing booking with a leisure and tourism facility. This kind of business is important to the facility and every effort should be made to make sure that the group is given some kind of special treatment to encourage it to keep coming back.

For instance, they might be given **exclusive** use of the facility at certain times of the day. A hotel, for example, might have signs in the reception area to welcome the group and offer it **complimentary** drinks or refreshments as part of the overall service provided.

THE JARGON DRAGON

exclusive – not shared with anyone else

complimentary – given free

People of different ages

No matter what type of leisure facility is involved, it is fair to say that the employees are likely to meet customers of all different ages. They will find that they have to adapt their manner accordingly. Younger people tend to be quite happy to be dealt with in an informal way but the older generation usually prefers a more formal approach and sometimes like to be called 'Mr' or 'Mrs' rather than by their first names.

THE JARGON DRAGON

concessionary – a reduced rate; these rates are often offered to students, young children and those over the age of 60 (women) and 65 (men) years

Sometimes those who have retired from work will receive **concessionary** entrance fees into leisure and tourism facilities. It should not be forgotten that they are still customers and are entitled to everything a full fare-paying customer has, as are students and younger children, who might also receive concessions.

FIND IT OUT

Ask your teacher if there are any local facilities that offer concessionary rates for groups of schoolchildren that he or she knows about. Now go back to the Alton Towers and Chessington World of Adventures websites and find out if they offer group discounts. How many individuals have to make up the group in order to qualify for this reduction?

People from different cultures

When we consider people from different cultural backgrounds we should remember that we are not simply talking about those from overseas or foreign visitors. We live in a multicultural society and leisure and tourism facilities need to remember this. Not only do they stand to lose valuable customers if they do not remember but they also risk breaking the country's laws against **discrimination**.

THE JARGON DRAGON

discrimination – treating someone unfairly

Sometimes people's cultural backgrounds affect the type of leisure activity they become involved in. A leisure facility that wishes to cater for all the different cultures that can be in one local area would need to consider this when designing the type of activities it has on offer.

They would also need to consider this if they sell food and drinks as part of the service they provide for their customers. Very often there are strict guidelines for people of different cultures about what they can and cannot eat and drink. If the facility is to offer the same customer service to all its customers then it needs to take these food and drink requirements into consideration and offer them in its restaurants, bars and cafés.

In many towns and cities in the United Kingdom you can find any number of people from different cultural backgrounds. The most common examples of different cultural backgrounds include:

- West Indians;
- Indians;
- Pakistanis;
- Africans;

- Chinese;
- Europeans;
- Turkish;
- Americans;
- Australians;
- New Zealanders.

Non-English speakers

The United Kingdom is attracting more and more visitors from overseas. Very often these are independent travellers and often they do not have a good command of the English language. Unfortunately only a small number of facilities in the United Kingdom offer a foreign language service to their customers. Much of the pleasure and understanding of visiting, for example, a place of historic interest, can be lost to the non-English speaking visitor if they are not guided around the site by someone who speaks their own language.

The following jobs are likely to require employees to have contact with non-English speaking customers:

- *tourist guides;*
- *waiters and waitresses;*
- *hotel staff;*
- *transport staff.*

Can you think of any more jobs that would come into contact, on a regular basis, with those visiting the country but unable to speak the language? If so, write a list and compare your list to those the rest of your class have made. Identify what languages they may need to be able to speak to do their job efficiently for all their customers.

People with specific needs

Providing good customer service means being able to cope with all eventualities or circumstances. Some customers have specific needs, including:

- Those with a disability that either restricts them to a wheelchair or makes it difficult for them to walk unaided.
- Those with a visual impairment, which means they do not have good eyesight and may need assistance.
- Those with a hearing impairment, which means they do not have good hearing and may need assistance.
- Those with literacy or numeracy difficulties, which mean they may not be able to read signs or notices and may need assistance.
- Those with dietary needs, which might include those with an allergy to some foods or those with diabetes. This could include those who do not eat meat (vegetarians and vegans) or those who cannot eat certain foods for religious reasons (for example Jews and Muslims).

Pregnant women and those with small children may also have specific needs. For example, they may not wish to use a swimming pool at very busy times. They may also need a nappy-changing room or facilities to warm milk or feed their babies.

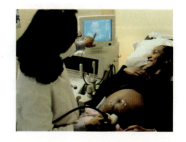

Think about the list of special needs we have given you. For each one we mention, write down how you think a leisure and tourism facility could help them. Now put your work onto computer and save your file as SPECIAL NEEDS.

There are some special signs related to these special needs that are used throughout this country, and in some other countries too. For example, signs showing where parking for disabled people can be found or signs showing where parent and child parking can be found. See if you can find some of these signs on the Internet and use them as images in your file.

Business men and women

As we discussed in Unit 1, businesses often use leisure and tourism facilities to hold meetings, conferences and conventions. A facility provides a package and will often provide a conference organiser to look after the arrangements for the business. This type of service to different business is known as a **corporate event**.

When a business or its employees attend a corporate event they are the customers of the leisure and tourism facility. They will, however, expect a very different service to an individual or group of customers, of whatever age group. They will be paying quite a large amount of money to the leisure facility for this service and they will expect the event to run very smoothly.

THE JARGON DRAGON

corporate event – an event in which a business organisation uses leisure and tourism facilities

The approach to the customers at such an event will have to be quite formal and usually all the arrangements are made through one representative of the business.

> *Go back to some of the websites you researched in Unit 1:*
>
> ```
> www.nationalsportscentres.co.uk/
>     bisham_abbey/index.htm
> ```
>
> ```
> www.nationalsportscentres.co.uk/
>     crystal/index.htm
> ```
>
> ```
> www.nationalsportscentres.co.uk/
>     hpp/index.htm
> ```
>
> ```
> www.nationalsportscentres.co.uk/
>     lilleshall/index.htm
> ```
>
> *and find out what conference and banqueting facilities they offer to businesses.*

External and internal customers

So far all of the different types of customer we have talked about are *external* to the organisation. This is because they are visitors to the leisure and tourism facility and come from outside it. External customers are vital to any organisation. They are the ones who pay to use the facility and without them the organisation cannot function.

The leisure and tourism facility will also have some *internal* customers. These are individuals or departments within the organisation itself and who work for the leisure and tourism facility. For example, the personnel section would make sure that enough trained staff are available, but the accounts or finance section would pay the staff.

People who work inside the leisure and tourism facility are also customers of the business. They work in order to provide themselves with an income and, in many cases, they rely on the business to provide them with opportunities to gain new skills and to develop and progress in their jobs.

In a smaller leisure and tourism facility there may only be a few employees, or internal customers. Each may answer the telephone and take messages for others. This makes communication and the passing on of information very straightforward usually and there is not too much of a likelihood that problems will occur.

Communication can be more complicated in a larger leisure and tourism facility. The organisation may well be divided into different departments and these may be situated on different floors, or even in different buildings. Members of one department or section are the internal customers of another department. This means that should one department require information from another it is just as important that the correct, accurate information is passed on. After all, all the employees are working for the same organisation, even if they are working in different departments.

Think
IT THROUGH

Think about your school. It has both internal and external customers. Produce a table with two columns. Head the two columns with the words 'internal' and 'external'. Now write a list under each heading of those who are internal customers of the school and those who are external customers. See if you can find out what kind of information they require from each other.

Benefits of customer service to leisure and tourism organisations

As we have already seen, leisure and tourism organisations have to respond to customer needs if they are to keep their customers. They also want to encourage new customers to visit their facility and they realise that if this is going to happen then they have to have a good image in the public's eye. In order to try to give their customers a good service they need to be employing staff who are trained to deal with a large number of different customer service problems.

Organisations don't just do these things for the sake of the customer. There have to be benefits to the organisation or they would not be prepared to spend time and money on providing the customer service. Let's look at why organisations want to provide good customer service and what benefits they get if they do so.

Increased sales

All leisure and tourism organisations exist in order to survive. This means that they have to make enough money to be able to pay their bills. Some of their biggest bills are:

- paying their staff (wages and salaries);
- buying the equipment they use (in a theme park, for example, this would be the rides);
- maintaining the equipment they use (having it serviced regularly in order to make sure it is safe).

What kind of equipment would your local library have to buy? What kind of equipment would your local gallery or museum have to buy? Try to identify some of the other costs the library, gallery or museum might have.

FIND IT OUT

Can you think of any more bills that a theme park would have to pay on a regular basis? If so, write a list of those you can think of and then discuss your ideas with the rest of your class.

THE JARGON DRAGON

expenditure – the money going out of a business

income – the money coming into a business

The paying of bills is what is known as an organisation's **expenditure**. They have to make sure that they make enough money to cover these items of expenditure from their **income**. A theme park's income would come from the entrance fees it charges its customers.

Obviously any organisation would want its income to be much greater than its expenditure so that it can make a **profit**.

income – expenditure = profit

To increase sales, a travel agent, for example, could sell car hire and foreign currency on top of the basic holiday package.

FIND IT OUT

1. *There are other ways in which a theme park could increase its income. Write down those you can think of and then discuss your ideas with the rest of your group.*

2. *From where would your local library obtain its income?*

3. *From where would your local gallery or museum obtain its income?*

See if you can work out how much profit you make. Write down your total income each week (this could be from pocket money, part-time job or any other money you get regularly). Then write down your total expenditure (this is what you spend the money on each week). Take the total expenditure away from the total income. If you've got money left at the end of the week this is your profit! If you haven't then you're not making a profit at all.

Often organisations put the profit they make back into the business to buy more equipment or improve their service to their customers.

So, one of the benefits to a leisure and tourism organisation of providing customer service is that they could increase the number of people using their facility and, therefore, increase their income.

THE JARGON DRAGON

profit – what is left from income after bills have been paid

Satisfied customers, repeat business and recommendations

Another benefit to the organisation of having an effective customer service provision is that its customers will be happy. If the organisation's customers are happy they will continue to use the facility. This is known as *repeat business*. The organisation will want their customers to keep coming back and to bring their family and friends along with them. If the service the organisation offers is good enough, this will happen and the business will benefit by having more customers.

The other benefit linked to repeat business is the fact that happy customers will recommend the organisation to people they talk to. If they receive a good service then they are likely to tell the people they work with and they may become customers themselves. So it goes on – if enough people recommend the business to their friends, relatives, work colleagues and others who may be interested in using the facility, then the number of customers will continue to increase. Repeat business and good recommendations to encourage new customers can only be good for any business.

eden project

A better public image

As we have already discussed in Unit 2, the image the general public has of a leisure and tourism facility is very important to the organisation. Many facilities spend a great deal of money on advertising in order to give the public a good image of themselves. They want the public to consider their facility as reliable, value for money and a good place to spend time, in a healthy and safe way.

Providing an effective customer service helps to project a good image to those who might be considering using the facility. If potential customers hear about the facility by recommendation from friends or family, then they will be more likely to use it themselves. If they hear many positive comments about the way the organisation provides advice, assistance and looks after their customers, then they are even more likely to be prepared to spend money at the facility.

Remember that people spend their leisure time in different ways. Leisure time is valuable to most of us and we are not often prepared to give it up. Not many people would choose to spend their leisure time at a place that has not got a good public image. They often only go to places that are popular with other people. At first they may just go to find out what it is like, but if they come away as happy customers then they will probably return. Remember also that customers need to feel confident about what a facility provides before they are likely to either use it or recommend it to others.

Go to the following websites (they are all sites you should have visited when studying Unit 1):

www.thebritishmuseum.ac.uk

www.ironbridge.org.uk

www.sciencemuseum.org.uk

From the information on these websites can you identify any ways in which the different organisations give a different public image? If so, what are the main ways each public image differs?

An edge over the competition

If an organisation is to succeed, it has to beat the **competition**.

There may be hundreds of other leisure and tourism facilities available to customers. There may even be several similar organisations in one local area.

If any one of those organisations is providing a better customer service than all the others, then it is more likely to attract more customers. Having more customers than your competitors gives you a distinct advantage over them.

THE JARGON DRAGON

competition – other businesses or organisations offering similar products or services

Think IT THROUGH

Are there any leisure and tourism facilities in your local area that have a reputation for being very good? Discuss this as a group and, if there are enough, come up with the top five that you can think of. What makes the first one better than the other four?

Having a reputation for not giving good customer service will act against the organisation. It will also give the competitors an edge over you. Every dissatisfied customer who reports your poor customer service is not only likely to use one of your competitors instead but is also likely to tell other people not to use you either.

A happy ending

Alun and Rosie had received several quotes from different travel agents of around £1900 for a package holiday. This was for a one-bedroom self-catering apartment in Majorca. Then a friend told them about a two-week holiday in a two-bedroom apartment in Santo Tomas on Minorca for £1650 with another, much smaller, independent local travel agent. They were delighted.

The whole holiday was wonderful. Airport transfers were in a small minibus, the resort representative had excellent local know-how without seeming too pushy, and the accommodation was lovely.

Their first experience of booking a holiday with a small independent company was one Alun and Rosie would totally recommend to their friends.

Not such a happy ending

When Jack and Hannah arrived at their resort of Benidorm, they discovered that the holiday bungalows they had booked were actually caravans. They ended up having to pay extra to the resort representative to change their accommodation.

They were taken to the hotel they had been transferred to, only to find that the place was filthy. Their room was very dirty and the air-conditioning unit made so much noise that they were unable to sleep. Several of the other rooms in the hotel were also burgled during their stay there.

Once again they asked the resort representative to move them somewhere else but they didn't get anywhere. The representative gave a rude and unhelpful response.

Jack complained when he got back to England and ended up with £1000 compensation from the national tour operator. However, his holiday had been ruined – he said he would never book with that company again.

Q1 *What would you look for in a holiday brochure to reassure you that customer service was important to the business? Identify one example of good customer service and one of bad customer service.*

Q2 *How might the local travel agent take advantage of the fact that Alun and Rosie were delighted with their holiday?*

Q3 *Put yourself in the position of the tour operator who provided Jack and Hannah with their holiday. You have just paid Jack and Hannah £1000 compensation. Last night, on television, Jack and Hannah appeared in a holiday programme and told the interviewer just how bad your company was. Suggest at least three things you should try to do to deal with this damage to your reputation and public image.*

Benefits of customer service to the staff and the organisation

Can you imagine how you would feel if you were an employee in the organisation that sold Jack and Hannah their holiday? We suspect that it would not be a particularly pleasant place to work at the time.

More pleasant place to work

We all hope to be able to do a good job for our employers. This isn't just for the sake of the employer but also for our own sake. If we can handle difficult situations well and cope with the work then we feel that we have actually achieved something. If the staff are providing a high level of service to one another, in other words supporting one another, carrying out jobs when they promised to do so and not letting one another down, then the staff will not only trust their colleagues, but there will be less tension within the workplace.

It is all too easy to blame another member of staff for not doing something when a customer makes a complaint.

Blaming others should be avoided as it may not be obvious why that member of staff did not do something which they promised to do. Or, for that matter, the customer may not be giving the correct version of the story.

Happier and more efficient workforce

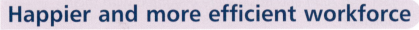

As we have already seen, employees need to be trained well and the organisation needs to have procedures in place for them to follow. If this is happening in an organisation, then the employees are likely to:

- feel that the organisation is a more pleasant place in which to work;
- feel happier because they have job satisfaction;
- be more efficient because they will have the confidence to deal with customers;
- feel valued by their employers;
- feel they are providing a quality service to the customers of the organisation;
- feel committed to the employers.

Improved job satisfaction

We all hope to have some *job satisfaction*. For some people, earning money is a job satisfaction but other people are hoping for something more than that. Enjoyment, even when the job is hard work and demanding, can give us satisfaction, particularly if we think that we are valued by our employers. In a leisure and tourism facility there are countless situations when customers need help and guidance. Being able to help them and receiving thanks from them is a positive step towards increasing job satisfaction.

If the leisure and tourism facility is providing an effective customer service provision, then the employees of that organisation will benefit in a number of ways; provided, that is, that the employees are looking for job satisfaction and are **motivated**.

Improved chances of promotion within the organisation

If employees feel valued and confident in doing their job, they will also feel that they have more chance of doing well within the organisation in the years to come. They are likely to stay longer with the same employer, rather than looking for another job. If they have spent a few months or years with the same employer and still feel confident and motivated, then they will feel that their chances of getting a better job within the organisation are improving.

Getting a better job within an organisation is known as *promotion*. Being promoted is another benefit to the employee because they will, perhaps, be given more responsibility at work and earn extra money for doing the new job.

FIND IT OUT

Look at the following list of possible reasons for achieving job satisfaction. Put them in the order that most matches your own needs. Put the most important thing for you first.

- *being paid well;*
- *having the chance of promotion;*
- *not having to work very long hours;*
- *getting praise for doing the job well;*
- *working with people I like;*
- *working alone;*
- *having a lot of contact with the general public;*
- *having a good boss;*
- *getting paid holidays;*
- *getting money off the organisation's products;*
- *having to wear a uniform;*
- *having the opportunity to do some more training.*

Did you have the list in the same order as other people in your class? Are there any other things that motivate you?

Communicating with customers

Now that we have a better understanding of how important customer service is to an organisation, we need to discuss the different ways in which employees can communicate with customers. These are:

- face-to-face, for instance when a customer comes to the organisation to make an enquiry, or even to make a complaint;
- over the telephone, possibly to ask for advice or information, or to make a complaint of some kind;
- in writing – by means of a letter or a price list;
- by computer – through the organisation's website or by email.

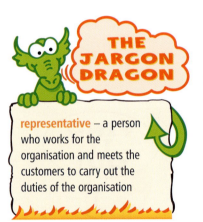

THE JARGON DRAGON

representative – a person who works for the organisation and meets the customers to carry out the duties of the organisation

Remember that however employees communicate with a customer they will always be viewed as the **representatives** of the organisation. Often a customer's impression of the organisation can be affected by the way they are dealt with by one single employee. The first impression that a customer receives of an organisation is very important, so whichever way the organisation has to communicate with customers, it is vital that the employees get it right.

Face-to-face communication

Face-to-face communication is probably one of the most important ways we all communicate every day. In any organisation there are many different face-to-face communications, including:

- Conversations which take place in the office or at a person's desk.
- Brief chats in the corridors or at lunch breaks in the canteen.
- Informal meetings – when one or two members of staff meet to talk about something.
- Formal meetings – when a group of employees are called together so that they can make some decisions or sort out a problem. Often at these meetings a secretary takes

notes so that there is a written record of what has been decided – these notes are known as the *minutes of the meeting.*

- When employees have contact with customers in person, say at a reception desk or at the counter of a shop.

- When a customer asks an employee for some advice, guidance or information. This may happen when the employee is just passing through a particular area of the organisation. Perhaps the customer might just want directions to another part of the organisation.

As we discover a little later in this section when we look at listening and speaking, there are a number of important things to consider when having a face-to-face conversation, or one on the telephone. These are:

- the way you speak – for example whether you make yourself clear, or whether you use slang during your conversation;
- the pitch and tone of your voice;
- the way you listen and pay attention to what is being said;
- knowing when not to speak or interrupt;
- knowing what questions to ask;
- being aware of body language – which can tell someone who can see you what you are thinking.

Body language is very important in face-to-face communication – more so than when speaking on the telephone because the two people having the conversation cannot see one another on the phone.

When having face-to-face communication with people a mixture of both verbal (spoken) and non-verbal (body language) communication is used. There are two considerations here:

- being able to read other people's body language;
- being aware that your body language can be read by the other person.

Let's look at body language in a little more detail:

- *Facial expressions* – these are the most common form of body language and we should always be aware of what our face is telling someone else. For example:
  - a smile can make a big difference when you meet someone;
  - our eyes can widen when we are surprised and narrow when angry;
  - our eyebrows move upwards when we don't believe something and lower when we are angry or confused about something;
  - we can look bored if our mouth is pouting.

- *Gestures* – we use our head and hands a lot when we agree or disagree with something. Remember that people from other countries often use their hands for making gestures more than us. Often what is an acceptable gesture in the United Kingdom is not acceptable in other countries or to people from those countries. Visitors to this country may not always understand our gestures. We can gesture to:
  - agree with someone by nodding our heads;
  - disagree with someone by shaking our heads from side to side;
  - waving our hands to greet someone from a distance;
  - pointing with our finger to give someone directions;
  - giving someone the 'thumbs up' sign to let him know everything is OK.

- *Posture* (the way we sit or stand) can also tell us a lot about what we are thinking or how we are reacting to someone else:
  - sitting well back in a chair with ankles crossed gives the impression of being relaxed or confident;
  - sitting on the edge of a seat gives the impression of being nervous;
  - standing straight with head high gives the impression of confidence;

– standing slumped with shoulders down gives the impression of being depressed or lacking confidence.

- *How close one gets to other people* – apart from shaking hands, we do not often come close to people we meet at work. Most people have an 'invisible circle' around them that they prefer others not to enter. This means that they may feel uncomfortable if others get too close to them. Getting too close to someone else's face can be a sign of aggression. Whether one is sitting or standing is also important. Someone who is seated and having a conversation with a person who is standing up can often feel 'lower' in importance than the one standing.

- *Eye contact* – one should always have eye contact with the person to whom one is talking. Eye contact shows the customer that the employee is giving them their full attention and often helps them to understand what is being said. Sometimes it is possible to get a better idea of how someone is going to react by looking into their eyes. Be careful though not to 'stare' into someone's eyes as this can be a sign of aggression.

When using face-to-face communication it is possible to see the other person's body language. Important considerations for face-to-face communication with customers are:

- be polite;
- be helpful;
- make them feel valued – try to use the customer's name during the conversation so they feel special and remembered;
- try not to be distracting by losing eye contact and looking elsewhere, or by fiddling with clothes or pulling at hair;
- let the customer finish the conversation;
- always leave with a smile and say 'goodbye'.

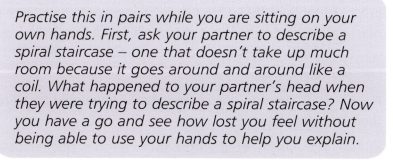

Practise this in pairs while you are sitting on your own hands. First, ask your partner to describe a spiral staircase – one that doesn't take up much room because it goes around and around like a coil. What happened to your partner's head when they were trying to describe a spiral staircase? Now you have a go and see how lost you feel without being able to use your hands to help you explain.

Think
IT THROUGH

case study

Body language speaks volumes

Up to 93% of communication is non-verbal, including your tone of voice, eye movement, posture, hand gestures, facial expressions and more. The pressure of body language can be felt in emotional situations especially. Body language usually prevails over words.

The *eyes* communicate more than any other part of the human body. Staring or gazing at other people can create pressure and tension in the room. Research suggests that individuals who can outgaze others develop a sense of control and power over others. Maintained eye contact can show if a person is trustworthy, sincere or caring. Someone who blinks too much can be seen as deceptive (not trustworthy or telling lies). People with eye movements that are relaxed, attentive and comfortable are seen as more sincere and honest.

Eyebrow muscles draw the eyebrows down and more towards the centre of the face if someone is annoyed.

The *smile* – it is believed that there are 50 or so different types of human smiles. Researchers can tell when a smile is true or whether someone is just smiling to be polite.

Hand and face *gestures* are just as important. Shrugging can give the impression of being deceptive or not caring. People who move their hands and arms about quickly while they are talking or touch items close by are also seen as probably telling lies. Gestures communicate – hand signals can communicate without the use of any speech. Touching communicates – touching can be friendly or it can be aggressive. The way people stand reflects their level of confidence and how comfortable they are in the situation.

Pausing a lot during a sentence and using the words 'uh' and 'um' frequently can give the impression of lying. So can failing to give a long enough answer to a question or to give an explanation when asked.

People need personal *space* and at times an individual can feel uncomfortable or threatened if another person comes into their personal space. Studies have shown that individuals who do not respect other people's space are less popular and are often rejected by others.

Note – if you want to win someone over you could try to copy their body language.

Q1 *What body language could help you guess whether someone is telling lies?*

Q2 *What body language could help you guess whether someone is relaxed in the situation they are in?*

Q3 *What body language would warn you that someone is getting annoyed?*

Q4 *What do you understand by the note at the end of the case study? You could try working in pairs and copying the body language of your partner to see if it works.*

Telephone communication

Dealing with telephone calls is different from face-to-face communication for the following reasons:

- explanations can only be in words as there is no body language to help reinforce what is being said;
- only the voice allows **attitude** to be expressed – this means that the way one speaks and phrases things is the only way that the caller is going to get an impression of attitude;
- voices on the telephone sound different from the way they do in a face-to-face conversation.

Telephone calls are very important to all organisations. A large booking for a leisure and tourism facility could be lost if the call is not taken in the most professional and efficient way. Those answering the telephone on behalf of the organisation should show a good *telephone technique*, which includes the following:

- Answer the telephone as quickly as possible and do not let it ring for ages before picking it up. If the person who normally answers is busy, someone else should answer their phone and help the customer in any way they can.
- The telephone should be answered with 'good morning' or 'good afternoon'. This is not just to be polite but it gives the caller the chance to realise that the phone call has started.

THE JARGON DRAGON

attitude – your view, feelings or opinion about something

- The name of the person answering, or the name of the organisation or department in which they work should be given. This allows callers to realise that they have got through to the right section and are talking to the right person.

- Form the habit of answering the telephone with the hand *not* used for writing. This leaves the writing hand free for jotting down any notes.

- Always have a pen and paper next to the telephone. Some organisations give their employees telephone message forms to use. These will have a series of different headings to help remind the employee about the questions they may need to ask the caller.

- If the telephone call means that you must obtain more information for the customer, then it may mean that the customer cannot be helped straight away. If this is the case the customer's name and telephone number should be taken and once what is needed has been found out, the customer should be called back straight away.

- If the telephone call is not for the person answering the call, those who answer should give the customers some options:
  - can someone else help them?
  - can a message be taken?
  - can someone else call them back when they are free to do so?

Some people forget how busy other people are once they get on the telephone. They talk for ages, giving lots of unnecessary information. This makes it more difficult for a person taking a message for someone else to pick out what is needed and what is not.

Have a look at the following telephone conversation.

Hello, my name is Diane. Can I speak to Mr Sutherland please? Oh he's not there. OK, well I should have telephoned about two hours ago but I went to do my weekly shopping and I met up with a friend of mine that I hadn't seen for ages. We went for a coffee and had a long chat and then when I got back to my car I realised I had forgotten to buy something from the supermarket so I had to go back in again. Anyway I don't really need to speak to Mr Sutherland but if you could just tell him that Clare phoned me today to say that his appointment for Friday week has been changed. She rang him at home because she had lost his works number – did I tell you I'm Mr Sutherland's wife? I know he thought he would have to go to see her at 11 but now its 12.30 instead. I don't know what the date is next Friday; perhaps you could look that up for me. Clare works for the local tourist board and he was meeting her about some advertising you want to do through them. Will you also tell him that the paperwork he was waiting for came in the post today? He also got that book he has been waiting for about Greece, but I suppose he'll have a good look at that when he comes home. We're having friends round for dinner tonight, but he might get a chance to look at it before they arrive. Thanks very much, you will tell him won't you? Bye.

Pick out the important parts of this message and write it out as if you were filling out a telephone message form for Mr Sutherland. Make sure you fill out the bottom part of the form, where you write your name, the date and time you took the message.

Written communication

A leisure and tourism organisation can communicate with its customers in writing. This written communication can take several different forms:

- Business letters – when the organisation writes to the customer or a number of different customers.

- A compliments slip, which could be included instead of a letter in, for example, a copy of the organisation's brochure.
- A brochure or catalogue, which would be glossy and expensive to produce – for example those held in travel agencies for tour operators. This would detail the products, services and other information about the organisation for the customer to browse through.
- A business card, which would be left by one of the representatives of the organisation. These are normally used to remind the customer of the name of the representative and the representative's telephone number or email address.

- Leaflets about the leisure and tourism facility.
- Displays in travel agents and at exhibitions about leisure and tourism.
- Advertisements about the organisation, including any special offers or discounts they may be using at the present time.
- Maps that might be included in brochures or sent out with leaflets, showing customers how to reach the organisation. Maps in a leisure and tourism facility itself might give customers information about the surrounding area and other attractions they could visit.

Business letters and letterheads

A business letter is a written communication sent to customers. These letters need to be neat, accurate and well presented. Leisure and tourism organisations will use headed paper as part of their **corporate image**.

The company letterhead will give the person who receives the letter the following details:

- the name and address of the organisation;
- the telephone number, fax number, email address and website of the organisation;
- the registered address of the organisation (this may be different from the postal address);
- the organisation's registration number (this is given to the organisation when it is first formed and is, in effect, the number of the company's 'birth certificate');
- the names of the directors or owners of the organisation;
- the names of any other companies or organisations with which the business has a relationship (such as membership of a professional organisation like the Association of British Travel Agents (ABTA) or the Association of Independent Tour Operators (AITO)).

THE JARGON DRAGON

corporate image – the way in which an organisation hopes to be seen and recognised by its customers and the general public

Does your school use letterhead paper? If so, ask your teacher for a copy and discuss what information this gives to people receiving a letter from a member of staff at the school.

Think IT THROUGH

The layout or format of a business letter will also be part of an organisation's corporate image and different organisations will have different rules about the way their letters are displayed. Usually a fully blocked method of display is used, which means that each part of the letter starts at the left-hand margin.

A business letter will contain all the necessary information in an attractively presented and accurate way. In addition to the information contained on the letterhead, there will be a date, a reference number and often a subject heading or a statement that says the letter is urgent or confidential.

Local Leisure

Susan Dodd,   Ref: 250150 Dec
17 Sampson Close,   15 March 2003
Huddersfield,
3HD 2SF

Dear Ms Dodd,

Horse Riding Lessons at the Leisure Centre

Yours sincerely,

PAUL MCNAMARA

FIND IT OUT

You have been asked to write a letter to a local travel agent who is going to come into your school to give a talk to the leisure and tourism students. The letter should include a map of your school and confirm the date and time of the visit, which is on 15 December at 11.00. Word process a letter to Ms Jennifer Gibson at Travel Ltd in your local high street. You can use your school headed paper if you are allowed. Remember to put a date on the letter and you can use the reference number LT/1512. Put your name at the bottom of the letter and sign it. Now hand it to your teacher for checking.

Logos and house styles

Most organisations have their own logo designed. This may be a simple drawing, a symbol or the fact that their name is always displayed in the same font and in a particular colour. Many businesses will have a logo and a catchphrase placed on each of their printed documents, always in the same place, perhaps in the top right-hand corner, or at the bottom, in the middle of each document. This is an easy way to maintain a corporate image and to make it absolutely clear from where the document has come.

How many logos can you think of without doing any research? Are there some that are in your mind straight away? Why do you think this might be the case? Draw those logos you can think of and, beside each, say why you think they are so easy to remember.

Think
IT THROUGH

Compliments slips

A compliments slip can look very much like the top of a business letter as it has all of the information usually found on a letterhead. Where it is different is its size (around a third of the size of a letter) and the fact that it has 'with compliments' pre-printed on it. Compliments slips are usually used instead of a letter and included in an envelope along with other information requested by a customer such as the organisation's brochure or price list.

Business cards

A business card again has elements found on a letterhead. Business cards have a named person who works for the business printed on them and they are used to help potential customers to contact that person by simply keeping the business card. They are usually printed on stiffer card so that they do not bend or tear. A modern development in business cards has been to print them on plastic (rather like a credit card) or even to produce a mini-CD that can then be put into a computer and by clicking on an email address or name a communication can be directly sent to the person who gave the digital business card.

Leaflets

Another way a leisure and tourism organisation would provide its customers and potential customers with information in a written form is by leaflets or flyers. Leaflets are a cheap way to send information to a large number of people. Organisations would sometimes pay people to post the leaflets through the houses in the local area, or they would use the following places to make them available to potential customers:

- tourist information centres;
- visitor information centres;
- libraries;
- town halls.

FIND IT OUT

Look in your local library, or in your local tourist information centre. Collect at least six different leaflets about different leisure and tourism activities that are taking place in the near future. For each of the leaflets decide:

- *Who you think they are designed for.*
- *What information is on the leaflets.*
- *Are they produced well – is the display good and do they make you notice them and want to read them?*
- *Is all the information contained on the leaflet clear and easy to understand?*
- *Do you need any more information about the activity or is everything contained on the leaflet?*

Choose one of the leaflets that you think is not very good. Can you make a better one yourself?

Posters

Posters are often placed in various sites around an area. They are used to publicise or advertise a leisure and tourism facility both to those who live in the area and visitors. The posters are usually produced by either:

- the leisure and tourism facility itself;
- the local transport company;
- the local tourist board;
- a tour operator.

Posters do not contain as much information as leaflets but just remind people that the leisure and tourism activity is about to take place. They give the date, time and details of where the event or activity is taking place.

Notices

Notices are a good way to pass on information to the visitor of a leisure and tourism organisation. They will normally be found in information centres at the site itself and may include:

- *Maps* of the surrounding area. Maps of the visitor attraction would show the layout of the site itself and possibly highlight the different areas so that visitors can clearly see where they are and where else they want to visit.

- *Timetables for local transport.* Information centres often provide timetables to cover all the public transport available in the area. Within the leisure and tourism organisation itself there may be different options of getting around the site. For example, there may be a train that tours the whole of a visitor attraction regularly, or there may be cable cars or monorail trains that take the visitor from one part of the attraction to another. The notice would give information about how often these forms of transport can be used and where they can be boarded.
- *Opening times* – these may not be just for the facility itself but could also be for other facilities in the local area.
- *Special events* – the facility may have a special event coming up that it hopes will appeal to many of its customers. These notices are often not very detailed and sometimes they are overprinted with words such as 'ONLY THREE DAYS TO GO' to make people notice them.

FIND IT OUT

Produce a poster or a notice to put on the wall of the leisure and tourism section of your school. This will inform all leisure and tourism students about a visit on 15 December from the travel agent. Make sure the poster is attractive and gives all the information the students need.

Language

The language which leisure and tourism staff should use when communicating with customers, either face-to-face, over the telephone or in writing, is often described as having to be 'professional'. Professional, in language terms, means avoiding using slang words such as 'mate' or 'see ya' when talking to customers, and avoiding using shortened versions of words such as don't, won't and can't.

As we have seen, there are a number of rules which staff are expected to apply to all situations when they communicate with customers. The overall impression that a customer needs to have of the organisation is efficiency, courtesy and a professional attitude.

Language is important and staff need to be aware that customers will need to be told the information not only in a clear and straightforward manner, but also in a way in which there can be no confusion as to what the communication actually means.

Pitch and tone of voice

One of the main things to remember whenever a member of staff communicates with a customer is that they should always remain calm. Staff should always try to ensure that they speak without resorting to shouting or speaking so fast that it becomes difficult for the customer to follow the conversation. There may be many situations, particularly in a leisure facility or a tourist attraction, when it is difficult to have a normal conversation with a customer, either face-to-face or on the telephone, because of background noise. If it is at all possible, conversations should take place where there is relative quiet so that a normal conversation can be had which does not require either the customer or the staff member to shout.

Using the right pitch and tone of voice when communicating with customers is a major part of being professional in the work situation. Being a true professional means always trying to be helpful and appearing enthusiastic, even when not necessarily feeling that way. The voice should not show irritation towards the customer, even if being asked a very obvious question for the twentieth time that day.

Pauses and silences

As we will see, listening and responding to customers means giving them a chance to say what they want to say, without rushing into giving them a quick answer. Each customer, no matter what type of leisure or tourism facility is involved, will expect to be treated as a valued customer. Staff should, therefore, listen and then respond only after the customer has finished what they are saying. Also, customers do not respond very well to being rushed into making decisions, so they should be given an opportunity to think before they respond. This means that staff should pause and wait for a customer to respond and be happy to remain silent while the customer makes their decision.

Body language

As we have already seen in the face-to-face communication section, body language is very important as it is the only situation where customers can actually see a member of staff. Much can be read into a member of staff's facial expressions, gestures, posture and eye contact.

Good body language reinforces a customer's impression that the member of staff is being helpful and polite. It shows that the customer is valued and that they are being listened to.

Poor body language can leave a very bad impression, not only of the member of staff but also of the facility itself. Even though the verbal information that may be being given to the customer is perfectly good and professional, poor body language, such as leaning against a wall or failing to maintain eye contact, can leave the customer feeling less than satisfied with the conversation.

Working accurately

Whether the written communication we send is a letter to our friend, an email to someone we know who lives in Canada, or a business letter, accuracy and the correct use of spelling and grammar are equally important. It is just as important that any written communication that leaves the organisation is accurate. The organisation wants to have a good public image. Its image could be lost if its written communications go out full of spelling or grammatical mistakes or if they are not presented to the customer in a professional way.

Although work produced by computer can be spell-checked using the software's facility, all work produced should be proofread. Note that spell-checks and other such technology can only be used effectively by an organisation if the employees are sufficiently well trained. It is important that employees know everything there is to know about how the software works and what it can do to help them complete their various tasks accurately.

Proofreading means reading the screen for errors before you print out the document and also checking the hard copy to ensure that none have been missed on the screen. This can take some practice and it is often a good idea to read the hard copy to a colleague as this reading process often highlights errors to both people.

Think IT THROUGH

The following text contains several errors. See how many you can find and then key it into a Word document, making sure you have corrected all the mistakes.

1 Usually a small some of money is kept in an ofice to pay for any odds and ends that may be needed. The persen in charge of this money may be called the Pety Casheer. It is his or her job to collect the money from the accounts Department every month. He or she keeps a strikt record of his it is spent, and totels up the petty cash book every month to make sure it is write.

2 'Petty" comes from the German word "petit" which means small, so you can see that the cashier doesn't handle large sums of money. Neverless, this money should never be left lieing about the office for anyone to take. It is usually left in alocked cash box. Before money can be issued, the cashier will want a singed Petty Cash Voucher. This states how much money the person is to recieve and what it will be used for. The voucher must be signed by someone in charge of the office

Listening and responding to customers

Because being able to concentrate and listen is so important, both for the organisation and for the customer, employees should be trained to make sure they are doing this. Listening is important both in face-to-face communication and for telephone calls.

We all listen to a great number of different people during one day but not many of us could remember exactly what has been said to us in each one of those conversations. That is why, when you are at work especially, it is a good idea to take notes during an important conversation. This helps you to remember what has been said later in the day.

How good a listener are you? In pairs, get your partner to tell you about a recent holiday or outing you have had. Your partner should talk to you for at least three minutes about this visit. Now you have to tell them back everything that you have remembered about their visit.

Did you remember most of it or did your partner have to remind you about some things? Now it is your turn to talk and your partner's turn to listen and then repeat back to you as much as he or she can remember about your visit.

It is important to make full use of our listening skills. To become a good listener:

- concentrate on what is being said;
- avoid becoming distracted, either by other people or by letting your attention drift elsewhere;
- don't let your mind wander onto other things;
- if your concentration lapses, then repeat the important words or phrases of the conversation in your head;
- look at the person speaking and respond by nodding or smiling;
- be ready for the other person to stop speaking – this is when it is most noticeable if one is not concentrating; a sudden silence can be embarrassing for both people;
- when the other person stops speaking, respond by commenting on what has just been said or by asking a question.

When we are listening to someone else during a face-to-face conversation, it is easy to respond by nodding or smiling to show we agree or understand, or frowning to show we don't really understand. This is not so easy to do when you are on the telephone.

Sometimes we have to ask a number of questions to make sure we understand exactly what is being said or what is required of us. Before we ask these questions though, we have to be sure of a few things, for example:

- Whether you are supposed to be asking questions. If you are not one of the important people in the conversation then it may be better to sit quietly and wait for the right time to ask an appropriate question.
- Whether the people in the conversation are interested and listening to what is being said. In a one-to-one conversation it is important to feel confident that the other person is listening.
- Will the people in the conversation be able to answer the question? The person asking the question has to be aware of the listener's own knowledge of the subject being discussed. It would be pointless to ask them any questions they are unable to answer.
- Is the question appropriate? It is important that the question or questions are related to the conversation. In the same way the question has to have a purpose, otherwise it would be pointless to ask it and it would be confusing for the other people in the conversation.

It is not always what is said that is important but how it is said. Whenever having a conversation with someone else, whether it is face-to-face or on the telephone, one should:

- not speak too quickly or too slowly;
- use the right words without being too complicated;
- listen to the comments that other people are making so to give the right response;
- show some confidence – confidence can be shown by:
  - looking at the other person;
  - smiling and looking positive;
  - never lying or stretching the truth;
  - actually answering the question and not causing confusion by talking about something else;
  - asking for the question to be repeated if there is misunderstanding;

- asking questions to help full understanding;
- trying to put the other person at ease so he has the confidence to say what he wants to say;
- thinking about what is being said;
- trying not to skip from one subject to another;
- not interrupting the other person.

Remember that a silence or pause in the conversation doesn't always mean that the other person has finished. It could be that they are thinking about what to say next or considering what they should do next.

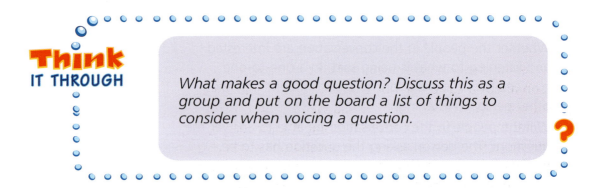

Think IT THROUGH

What makes a good question? Discuss this as a group and put on the board a list of things to consider when voicing a question.

Asking appropriate questions (open and closed questions)

There are many different types of questions a person can ask to obtain more information in a customer/employee situation. They can be divided into *closed questions*, where the person answering might only need to say 'yes' or 'no' in reply, and *open questions,* where you ask a question that requires the other person to give more than a 'yes' or 'no' answer.

Examples of closed questions are:

- Did you have a nice time at the theme park?
- Will you be home at the usual time?
- Do you have enough money?

Examples of open questions are:

- Which rides did you go on at the theme park?
- What time do you expect to be home?
- How much money have you got?

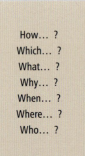

How… ?
Which… ?
What… ?
Why… ?
When… ?
Where… ?
Who… ?

Open questions usually start with the words shown on the left.

Think
IT THROUGH

Put the following closed questions into open questions by starting with the right words.

1. Did you enjoy school today?
2. Did you go out at lunchtime?
3. Was the bus on time?
4. Did you see many people at the cinema that you knew?
5. Have you eaten much today?

Obviously, employees who are trying to find out more information about a customer would prefer to receive a longer reply than just a 'yes' or 'no'. They would want to encourage the customer to give them full answers. Using silence can encourage thought in someone else. If a question is asked and someone gives a quick and short answer, by remaining silent it is possible to make the speaker realise that he hasn't said enough and that he needs to add to what he's already said.

Using *follow-up questions* can also help you to obtain as much information as possible. To get the most information it is not a good idea to ask question after question. Stick to one subject and ask a few questions about that before moving onto something else.

Whatever type of question is asked:

- It should be clear to the other person so that the customer understands what is being asked.
- It should not repeat something that has already been asked or ignore something that the other person has already said.
- It should be asked using the right tone of voice. The way one asks can make it sound completely different. Be careful not to sound sarcastic or give the impression of 'taking the Mickey' when asking a question. Don't try to be funny either – people have different senses of humour and one person's idea of funny might not be the same as another's.
- It should be asked at the right time – never butt in or interrupt when someone else is speaking.

Personal presentation

For leisure and tourism organisations, whose employees have direct contact with their customers, it is important that the staff look presentable. If they wish to represent a company in the best way, employees would have to think about the following:

- the way they dress for work;
- their personal hygiene;
- the way they behave when they are at work;

- their personality – whether or not they are often grumpy or sometimes a bit too loud;
- their general attitude when they are at work – whether or not they look as if they are approachable and how they treat other people.

Think
IT THROUGH

Look at the list above. Why do you think all of these considerations are important? Give reasons for your answers.

Dress

Some people are fortunate enough to be issued with a uniform that they have to wear for work. This may not seem very fortunate to you but once you start work you will realise just how important it is that you dress in the right way.

Uniforms are issued by some organisations for a number of reasons, including:

- they form part of the company image in that the uniforms may have the company logo printed on them;

- employees will always be easy for the customer to find because they will all be wearing the same clothes;

- it means that they do not have to pay their employees an allowance for their work clothing;

- it means all their employees will turn up for work in the appropriate clothes and, hopefully, they will all look smart and well presented.

If an individual doesn't work for an organisation that issues a uniform, then he or she will be expected to dress in clothes appropriate to the job. This means as smartly and as tidily as possible. Very often leisure and tourism organisations insist on certain dress codes. These are rules about what can or cannot be worn for work. Some of them are based on health and safety reasons:

- long hair needs to be tied back if the job involves working with food;

- no nail varnish can be worn when food is being handled or prepared;

- dangling jewellery should not be worn in case it gets tangled in equipment or machinery;

- those who run rides, for example, have to wear safety equipment like hard hats, goggles or waterproof clothing.

As well as health and safety clothing, sometimes organisations insist that their employees wear their name tags on their clothing or wear their pass. These name tags and passes are worn for security reasons, to try to make sure that only authorised people enter certain areas of the organisation.

What is chosen to wear for work very much depends on the job being done. For instance:

- some organisations insist that male employees wear a collar and tie to work;
- some organisations do not allow their female employees to wear trousers – very often this is the case for air cabin crews.

FIND IT OUT

Visit your local leisure centre and your local travel agent. Note down what the staff of each of these organisations are wearing. Do you think they are issued with a uniform? Is it easy to recognise who the employees of the organisation are?

Now write down what you think are the advantages and the disadvantages to an individual who has to wear a uniform for work. Perhaps a member of your family or a friend has to wear a uniform. If so, ask them what they think the advantages and disadvantages are.

Personal hygiene

Whatever clothes are worn for work, there is another consideration about what is being worn. It is how clean the clothes are. It would be useless for an organisation to give its employees a uniform to wear if they arrived for work with stains on their trousers or tops.

Very few people have money to spend on new clothes all the time, but if they are washed regularly and taken care of, it shouldn't be necessary to keep buying new ones. Clean clothes, clean hair, cleaned shoes and a clean body all add up to being presentable. Personal hygiene doesn't just mean cleaning your teeth and having your wash, bath or shower in the morning. It includes your clothes.

- Clothes should always be clean and changed daily.
- Personal hygiene is important – shower or bath daily and use a good antiperspirant deodorant. If perfume or an aftershave is used, make sure it is not too strong smelling.
- Females should not apply make-up too heavily.
- Shoes should be clean and sensible.
- Hair should be neat and clean.
- Fingernails should be neat and clean.
- Oral hygiene (the mouth) is also important. Teeth should be cleaned every morning and a pack of mints should be kept handy to freshen the breath.

Personality, attitude and behaviour

There are many different ways of looking at these three aspects of a member of staff. The fact is that the three aspects are very much related to one another. An individual's personality will often determine their attitude to work and their behaviour whilst at work. For many years researchers have been looking at personality and how this affects behaviour and attitude. Most seem to have come to the same conclusion; that there are five main factors which determine an individual's personality. These are:

- Conscientiousness – being conscientious means being happy to be busy and taking a pride in the quality of work that is done.
- Neuroticism – being neurotic means that the individual is very nervous of situations, particularly ones which might cause them problems or give them difficulty in dealing with. It is quite common to be nervous the first time something new has to be done, perhaps talking to customers without help for the first time, or having to deal with a problem on one's own for the first time. This really is a measure of how a member of staff copes with these situations after they have had their training and have experienced situations like this before.
- Extroversion – being an extrovert can often mean that an individual is loud, outgoing, confident and never really bothered with what they are asked to do because they feel able to do most things. Many leisure and tourism organisations like to employ extroverts, as customers are

often more comfortable with someone who is outwardly confident and enthusiastic.

- Agreeableness – being agreeable is a measure of a person's ability to get on with other people in a variety of situations. It is therefore a measure of someone's ability to work with others in a team, or to share work, or to get on with customers. It is not just being likeable; it is also about being adaptable and flexible.
- Openness – being open means being approachable, truthful and honest and having an ability to get along with others.

As the majority of jobs in leisure and tourism require staff to deal with customers on a day-to-day basis, the organisations will look for individuals who have the right kind of personality, attitude and behaviour to work.

It is often common for staff to come to work feeling tired, irritable or unhappy. But it is a measure of a person trying to do a professional job that none of these negative attitudes come out in behaviour in front of customers.

Handling complaints

In carrying out their business activities, many leisure and tourism facilities will receive a number of written complaints from their customers. As we already know, the organisation will want to act on complaints that it receives. They will use the complaints to try to improve the customer service provision.

In response to a letter of complaint, the organisation would have to write back to the customer. Depending on the type of complaint, this could be a simple letter of apology that it will send to the customer, or it could involve any of the following:

- the letter plus an offer of some type of refund of money spent by the customer;
- the letter plus an offer to replace faulty products or services bought by the customer;
- the letter plus an offer of a cash payment to pay the customer back for any problems or inconvenience that they have had.

Obviously an investigation into the complaint would have to be undertaken by the organisation. It would be interested in finding out whether the complaint was a result of some action by an employee or group of employees. If this was the case, then the organisation would want to reassure the customer that the individual would be suitably disciplined.

Even if, after its investigations, the organisation discovers that the customer has no real cause for complaint, it would still want to respond to the customer. Often it would:

- apologise to the customer for the fact that he or she found cause to complain;
- make a 'token' offer to the customer. This could be a voucher to be spent at the organisation in the future. It would do this so that the customer felt satisfied with the way the organisation had handled the complaint. The organisation would do this to maintain 'goodwill' with the customer.

All letters of complaint should be handled as quickly as possible. Even when an enquiry or investigation has to be undertaken before a solution is found, the customer should be kept informed as to what the organisation intends to do and when it intends to do it.

Have you had any reason to write a letter of complaint to an organisation about anything? Discuss this as a group.

Think IT THROUGH

FIND IT OUT

Working with a partner, read the following situation:

> *You have arranged a birthday party for your nephew at your local leisure centre. You were assured that the group of children and supervising adults would have the place to themselves. You have paid the deposit for the party. On the day of the party you all arrive, only to find that you do not have exclusive*

FIND IT OUT

use of the facility but that another birthday party is taking place in the next room.

Both you and your partner should now write a letter of complaint to the leisure centre. Now hand your letters of complaint to another pair of students. Read the letters of complaint your fellow students have written and respond to both of them in writing. Make sure you check your work before handing it back to them.

Not all complaints received by a leisure and tourism facility arrive in the mail or in writing. Customers may, of course, wish to make a complaint whilst they are at the facility. This would require dealing with the problem face-to-face. Alternatively they may decide to complain once they get home, in which case the complaint could have to be handled during a telephone conversation.

Many of the ways in which a complaint can be resolved in a written situation apply to both face-to-face and telephone complaints. The major difference, however, is that the complaint has to be handled 'live', and therefore the member of staff needs to be able to think on the spot, make decisions immediately, or pass the customer on to a more senior member of staff.

Many of the points which were dealt with in the face-to-face communication and telephone communication sections earlier in this Unit therefore apply in complaint situations. It must always be remembered that something must have gone wrong as far as the customer is concerned in order for them to be complaining. In other words, the issue is important to them, although it may not appear to be important to the member of staff having to deal with the complaint.

Politeness at all times is important; otherwise the situation may get out of hand and become far more serious. It is also important for the member of staff to listen carefully and to show an interest in what the customer is saying. It may be just as important that the member of staff notes down the important points in the complaint, particularly if the matter has to be referred to a more senior member of staff.

In most cases a minor complaint can be dealt with on the spot by an apology or a reassurance that something will be done in the future. Other complaints may be more complicated and may require the facility to send the customer a written explanation and apology once the situation has been investigated. At all times the customer needs to be told what will happen and who will be handling the complaint, as well as when they can expect some kind of answer.

Keeping customer records

Another important way that any organisation can provide an effective customer service provision is to keep accurate and up-to-date information about its customers. The organisation will want to know as much as possible about its customers so that it can provide them with exactly what they need.

The different types of leisure and tourism organisations often keep customer records for different reasons:

- *Health clubs,* for example, would keep details of their customers' names, addresses and telephone numbers but they would need to keep on record any medical information that has to be considered about individual customers. They would use this information to provide the customer with their own personal fitness plan.

THE JARGON DRAGON

confidential – something secret or private to the organisation that should not be seen by others

Obviously, if this medical information is on file within the health club then it is vital that this is kept **confidential** and, even more importantly, that it is absolutely accurate. Health clubs, like most organisations in the leisure industry, will need their customer records in order to know when memberships need to be renewed. They would also hold bank details about customers who pay their membership fees on a monthly or yearly basis.

- *Travel agents* would also keep details of customers' names, addresses and telephone numbers. But they would not necessarily need any medical details.

Think IT THROUGH

Discuss as a group what could happen if a health club had on record the wrong information about someone's medical history.

?

They would want to know where the customer has been on holiday in the past, at what time of year they tend to go on holiday and how much they usually pay for their holiday. The travel agent would use this information to contact the customer slightly before the time they usually book their holidays.

FIND IT OUT

Write down why you think:

- *the travel agency would benefit by contacting customers early;*
- *the customer would benefit by being contacted early.*

Sometimes organisations use customer records for **marketing** purposes.

They try to obtain customer information so that they can:

- find out how often they spend their money (their spending habits);

- find out what they like to spend their money on (their tastes);
- record how often they visit the organisation and what they spend their money on while they are there;
- find out what they intend to spend their money on in the future.

If organisations have the above information about their customers, or potential customers, together with their names and addresses, then they can make sure the products and services they offer meet their needs. This will help them to keep their existing customers and attract new ones. It will also help them to ensure that they have an edge over their competitors.

THE JARGON DRAGON

marketing – getting the right product to the right people in the right place at the right price using the right promotion

Think IT THROUGH

Think back to what we said earlier about gaining an edge over the competition. Why would organisations want to do this? Discuss this in pairs and then write down what conclusions you have come to. Now tell the rest of your class what you and your partner have decided.

Leisure and tourism organisations might keep their customer records on index cards. These are postcard-size pieces of card that are filed in a small filing cabinet. This means that each time they find out about a new potential customer, they add an index card to the file. The index cards could be filed in alphabetical order. However, they probably keep the information in a computerised **database**.

THE JARGON DRAGON

database – this is a way of keeping a lot of different pieces of information on a computer

Fold a sheet of A4 paper in half and then into half again. Cut the paper along the folds to give you four card-sized pieces of paper. Repeat this until you have 16 card-sized pieces. Now ask 16 people in your class for their names, addresses, telephone numbers, date of birth and preferred leisure activity.

FIND IT OUT

FIND IT OUT

1. *Sort them in alphabetical order (the first letter of the surname tells you where they should be placed).*

2. *Now select only those who have a birthday in June.*

3. *Now choose one of the most popular leisure activities and select only those people who choose to do that activity.*

Keep these index cards safe because you are going to find out in the next activity how much easier it is to do this task using a computerised database.

The computer software can make life much simpler and save lots of time, for example it can:

- sort the names into alphabetical order;
- select just those people of a certain age group;
- select just the males or just the females;
- select just those people who live in a particular area of the region;
- select just those people whose membership needs renewing in April.

Microsoft Access database software

- allows the user to store information (data) in the form of records relating to one individual or item;

- allows the person who sets up the database to decide exactly what will be included by setting up different sections known as *fields*;
- allows information entered into the database to be sorted in a variety of different ways;
- allows information to be taken from the database as a list, an individual record, a group or just one section of all of the records;
- allows the data to be copied into other Microsoft software formats, such as Word or Excel.

Creating customer records

Each piece of information in a database is known as a *field*. Each field will be given a title. It will then be necessary to say how much information is likely to be put into that field. Having identified the title of the field and the length it is required to be, it is then necessary to identify what type of information will be put into this field.

By type of information, we are considering what the computer will be able to recognise and deal with. When deciding on the size of fields to be included it is best to remember that the computer has only limited memory. For this reason it is not a good idea to make the fields too long, but to allow enough space for the information to be entered. The following are field types:

- *Text* – letters, numbers and symbols.
- *Numbers*.
- *Dates* – it is possible to insert dates into a field so that renewal dates and diary entries can be made. You could then search for all those born on a certain date. A date format will appear as: –/–/–.
- *Time* – these fields will appear in the same way as the date format.

So it is possible to create fields that take the following types of information:

- surnames (text);
- first names (text);
- addresses (text and numbers);
- postcodes (text and numbers);
- dates of birth (date);
- telephone numbers (number);

- age (number);
- medical information (text);
- renewal of membership date (date).

When you open Access you will be presented with the window shown above. Choose one of the first two options if you are creating a new database. You must save an Access database before you start working on it. After choosing BLANK ACCESS DATABASE you will be asked to choose a location and a name for the database, as shown below.

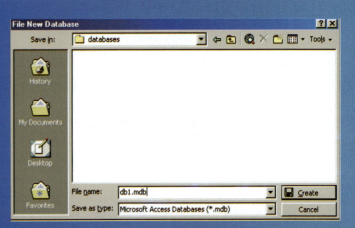

Find the folder where you want to save the database in the SAVE IN drop-down menu, then key in the name of the database in the FILE NAME line and then click on the CREATE button. You then get the following screen and you should choose CREATE TABLE IN DESIGN VIEW:

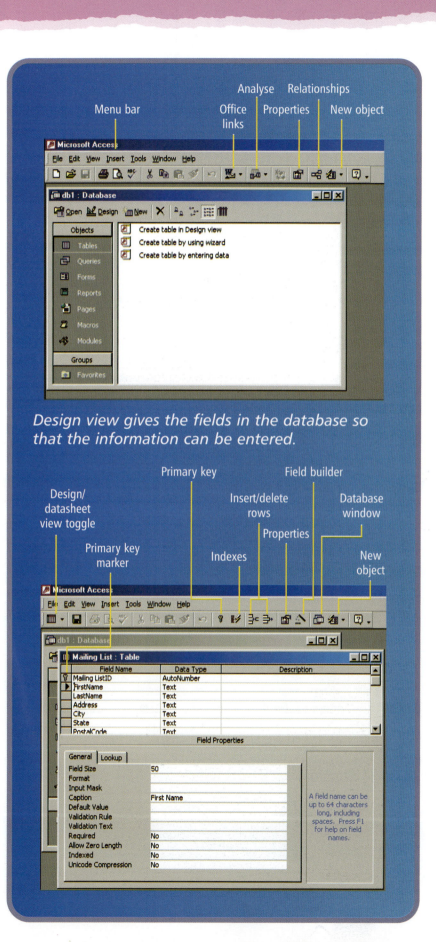

Menu bar — Office links — Analyse — Properties — Relationships — New object

Design view gives the fields in the database so that the information can be entered.

Design/datasheet view toggle — Primary key — Field builder — Insert/delete rows — Database window — Primary key marker — Indexes — Properties — New object

Create your database in design view with the following fields:

- *name;*
- *date of birth;*
- *telephone number;*
- *main activity.*

Make sure you have saved the database properly and that all the information you have put into the field headings is correct. You will need this database again so be careful that you are accurate.

Once the design of the database has been finished, you can then key in the different information about each of the customers. These pieces of information make up what is known as a *record*.

You can now go back into Access and this time you can choose OPEN EXISTING TABLE.

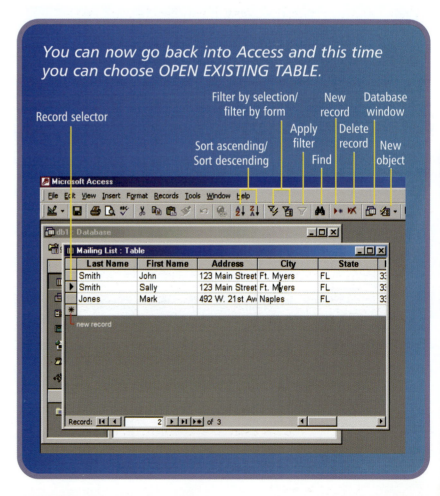

The DATASHEET (as shown in the illustration above) shows the field names you chose in the last activity as column headings (in the grey section at the top of each column, which goes down the datasheet). Each row (going across the datasheet) is an individual RECORD. The datasheet allows you to enter data onto the database.

This is where you need the information that you put on your index cards. Key in, under the right field headings, the information about eight of your classmates. They do not have to go into the database in any special order because you are going to change it slightly later.

Once you have done this you will see that you have a database containing eight records.

When you are in datasheet view, if you decide you need to change the title of a field, or the length of the field, then you can click on the 'toggle' icon and it will take you back to design view.

Finding and changing existing records

You can add a new record to your database when you are on the datasheet by keying in the new record beside the asterisk. You can also click on the NEW RECORD button at the bottom of the datasheet to move to the last blank record.

Go back into your database and add the records for your other eight classmates. Your database will now contain a total of 16 records.

FIND IT OUT

It is easy to make changes to records you have already put into a database. This is known as *editing* records. To edit records you just have to place the cursor in the record that is to be edited and make the necessary changes.

You can also use the FIRST, PREVIOUS, NEXT and LAST buttons at the bottom of the datasheet to help you move through it.

You can remove (delete) a record on a datasheet by placing the cursor in any field of the record row and selecting EDIT/DELETE RECORD from the menu bar or by clicking the DELETE RECORD button on the datasheet toolbar.

You can also add extra columns and delete columns. You can add them quickly in the datasheet by highlighting where you want the new column to go in the grey area at the top of the datasheet. You then choose INSERT, then COLUMN, from the menu bar. Columns can also be deleted by placing the cursor in the grey area at the top of the column and selecting EDIT and then DELETE COLUMN from the menu bar.

FIND IT OUT

You now find out that you only need 12 records on your database. Decide which four records are not going to be useful to you later and delete them from the 16 records you already have.

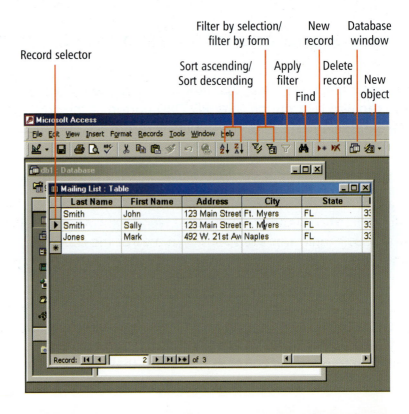

It is possible for you to view records in a different way using Access. You can change the order of the records and you can select only those records that match what you are looking for. Let us look at this in more detail.

Sorting is the way you would change the order of your records. You can sort records by date or by alphabetical order. You highlight the column you want to sort by placing the cursor at the top of that column and clicking. You can either choose RECORDS then SORT then SORT ASCENDING (A first) or DESCENDING (Z first) from the menu bar or take the short cut by clicking on the icon below.

Go back into your database and print a copy of all your records as they are at the moment.

Now you are going to sort them into alphabetical order. Click at the top of the NAME field to highlight the column then click on the icon shown below.

Has it changed the order of the records? If so, print a copy of your sorted database.

You can *select* records from your database that include only the information you require. For instance, you might want to select just those people who live in a certain area of the country or who like a particular activity. In order to select these records you would:

Place your cursor in the field that you want to filter the records by and click the FILTER BY SELECTION icon on the toolbar (as shown below).

Queries select records from tables in a database. To create a query you have to be in the design view. From the QUERIES PAGE on the window, click on the NEW button, then select DESIGN VIEW and click OK. Then select TABLES AND EXISTING QUERIES from the TABLES AND QUERY TABS then click the ADD button to add each one to the new query.

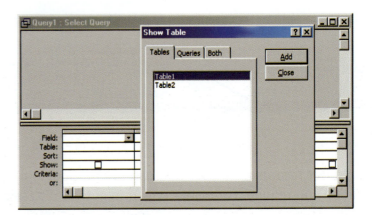

Click CLOSE when the table and queries have been selected. You can add fields from your saved table to the new query by clicking on the field name in the TABLE BOX or by selecting from FIELD and TABLE.

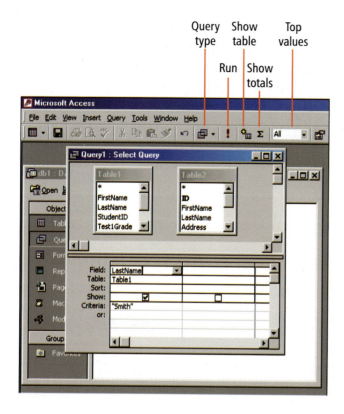

You put your query into the CRITERIA field. For example, you could key in 'FOOTBALL' or 'CINEMA' or 'COMPUTER GAMES' in the activity column to find those who have said this is their favourite activity.

Using Access you can take out records of only those of your classmates who like your favourite activity. You have to do this by creating a query in design view of the database. Follow the instructions we have given you above and see if you can find just those who like to do your favourite activity. If you are successful print a copy of your query.

You should now be able to see how much easier it is for leisure and tourism organisations to keep their customer records on a computer than on index cards. Using a computer does not just help the organisation, it also helps the customer.

How much longer do you think it took you to sort out your records by hand than it did using the computer? Can you imagine how much longer it would take if there were thousands of different records? What if there were more fields involved?

Accuracy and confidentiality

Accurate information is important. The organisation is not so likely to make mistakes using a computer – provided, of course, that the person keying in the information is trained to do so.

Keeping customer records accurate and safe is vital. An organisation will try to make sure that only certain employees can see the customer records because they are *confidential*. This would be for the benefit of the customer, so that nobody else can find out their details, but it would also be for the benefit of the organisation, which would not want to let its competitors know about their customers. Another reason is that there is now a legal requirement under the Data Protection Act for organisations to keep any information they store on computer about their customers confidential.

Look on the Internet and see what you can find out about the Data Protection Act. How does it protect customers?

If customer records are kept on computer, an organisation can make sure they remain confidential in a number of ways, including:

- ensuring its staff have to use a *password* to use the computer system.
- ensuring their staff have **screen-savers** so that they don't leave confidential material on their computers when they are away from their desks;

- ensuring that computers are not situated in public areas of the organisation – for instance the reception area or other places where the general public can see the screens.

THE JARGON DRAGON

screen-saver – a moving image on the computer screen that appears if the computer is not used for a few minutes

Think
IT THROUGH

You might have to use a password to use your school's computers, even if it is to do your own work. Why do you think schools make students do this? How does using a password keep your work confidential?

Think
IT THROUGH

We've explained how to help keep information confidential when using a computer. Can you list the ways you could help to keep your handwritten index cards confidential? Think about when you are away from your desk. Think about what you say to other people. These are very important when looking after information about other people. What else can you think of?

case study

The best of English tourism announced

The English Tourism Council (ETC) announced the 32 shortlisted finalists in the Safeway Excellence in England Awards 2002. The finalists were competing for the awards, which honour the United Kingdom's:

- best visitor attractions (large and small);
- best hotels (large and small);
- best self-catering holiday accommodation;
- best caravan park;
- best bed and breakfast accommodation;
- best tourist information centre;
- most improved resort;
- individual who has provided the most outstanding customer service.

The key points being tested included a commitment to:

- excellent accommodation or facilities;
- high standards of customer service;
- care for the environment;
- clever business ideas to attract new customers and to encourage repeat business;
- accessibility for disabled guests.

Judges' comments about the winners and why they won

Bed and breakfast of the year
Clow Beck House
Monk End Farm, Croft-on-Tees, Darlington DL22 2SW

This has everything, the views, the warm welcome, memorable service and great food, and all at a competitive price. They really care about their guests. This B&B has 13 luxurious *en suite* rooms, all individually decorated with antiques. Service is second to none and nothing is too much trouble. Guests can enjoy excellent home-grown food served in a magnificent beamed dining room. The breakfast menu is extensive and includes home-made bread and preserves and free-range eggs. Guests with disabilities are also well catered for and one of the bedrooms has been fully adapted to be wheelchair accessible.

Caravan holiday park of the year
Kelling Heath Holiday Park
Weyborne, Holt, Norfolk NR25 7HW

This caravan park is leading, not following, and it is listening to its customers. The park is set amongst 250 acres of woodland and heather in an area of outstanding natural beauty and offers a truly memorable experience to all its customers. Visitors can either stay in a luxurious holiday home with central heating, shower room and well-equipped kitchen, or bring their own caravan or tent and use the high-quality on-site facilities. The park has an excellent leisure club with a pool and gym, and guests can enjoy the sympathetically managed natural environment with nature trails, cycle routes and night walks to see the bats and the stars.

Hotel of the year (under 60 bedrooms)
Matfen Hall Hotel
Matfen, Newcastle upon Tyne, Northumberland NE20 0RH

This hotel is a great idea, providing an outstanding experience for guests. It is a magnificent country house hotel set in the heart of some of the most picturesque countryside. This mansion has been sympathetically restored and most of its original features remain. Each of the 30 bedrooms combines the most up-to-date facilities with traditional elegance, and the executive rooms are particularly spacious with their own dining areas and luxury bathrooms. Guests can relax in the drawing room or dine in the fine library restaurant, which serves contemporary English cuisine using local produce. The hotel also has its own golf course.

Hotel of the year (over 50 bedrooms)
Island Hotel
Tresco, Isles of Scilly, Cornwall TR24 0PU

This lovely English beach hotel provides an experience that surpasses all expectations. It is an ideal family hotel set on the unspoilt island. Guests, who arrive both by boat and by helicopter, are met by a tractor-drawn open bus and are greeted personally by the general manager. The hotel itself is right on the beach and has sea views. Each of the bedrooms is beautifully decorated and service at the hotel is outstanding. There is a particularly high number of staff and all are highly trained in customer service. There is an excellent restaurant where local fish is a speciality.

Most improved resort of the year
Scarborough
North Yorkshire

Over the last few years, this resort has undergone a renaissance as a seaside resort thanks to a huge range of initiatives that have improved every aspect of the town for visitors. These include improving the quality of accommodation by introducing a new inspection of accommodation in the town. The seafront has also been greatly improved – shop fronts have been restored, trees planted and new lighting installed, signs and local information have been updated and a new tourist information centre has been opened on the seafront.

People Award for Outstanding Customer Service
Stephen Hallam
Managing Director, Dickinson and Morris 'Ye Olde Pork Pie Shoppe and The Sausage Shop', 8–10 Nottingham St, Melton Mowbray, Leicestershire LE13 1NW

A traditional piece of England has been marketed very well by giving excellent customer service. All shops and services in England are part of tourism and this person works at county and regional level to further tourism's interests. He has an excess of energy and enthusiasm that inspires those around him. His capability is outstanding, and his customer awareness and service are exemplary. He manages to lead his operation personally, meeting customers and working alongside his team to encourage their very best efforts. He is an excellent role model and a superb ambassador for the industry.

Self-catering holiday of the year
Underscar
Fisherbeck Mill, Old Lake Road, Ambleside, Cumbria
LA22 0DH

A beacon of quality that could tempt people to turn their backs on Portugal as their holiday destination! This property offers luxurious accommodation, excellent facilities and a passionate commitment to the environment. These five-star self-catering and leisure properties are modern units sleeping from two to eight people. It has excellent conservation and energy-saving practices in place and is involved in local conservation projects including one scheme to help fund a person to maintain footpaths in the area.

Tourist information centre of the year
Liverpool Tourist Information Centre
Queen Square Centre, Roe St, Liverpool, Merseyside L1 1RG
Albert Dock Tourist Information Centre
Atlantic Pavilion, Albert Dock, Liverpool L3 4AE

This is an energetic and up-to-date tourist information centre. It is proactive, constantly trying out new ideas and using the latest technology. Staff development and training is excellent. It aims to provide an unrivalled service by investing heavily in staff training and using new technology such as text messaging and email to boost business to the city.

Visitor attraction of the year (over 100 000 visitors)
Science Museum
Exhibition Road, London SW7 2DD

This museum is everything a great tourist attraction should be – there is something that appeals to all ages. Excellent new developments have helped the museum keep its edge over the competition. The museum is constantly updating its galleries and developing innovative exhibitions. It houses six cutting-edge exhibitions, has colour-coded floors, an excellent team of staff and provides visitors with a wealth of information.

case study

The best of English tourism announced

Visitor attraction of the year (under 100 000 visitors)
The World of Glass
Chalon Way East, St Helens, Merseyside WA10 1BX

This is a terrific example of a tourist attraction. This attraction demonstrates quality in all areas. Visitors can experience live demonstrations, and watch an audio-visual show, as well as exploring the past. The whole visitor experience from interpretation to catering is outstanding and there is an excellent shop selling a range of products.

Short break destination of the year
Northumbria

This area is famous for its castles and golden beaches, as well as its open moorland and green farming country. It is one of the few English regions that has large expanses of untouched countryside, such as the national parks and the areas of outstanding natural beauty. In contrast, it also has lively cities that offer visitors the best choice of shopping and eating out. There are also historic and cultural attractions. The diversity of scenery and variety of attractions makes this underrated region a deserving winner. It has wild and wonderful countryside and offers a fantastic English experience. It has an enticing combination of heritage, romantic castles and rugged coastline. It just goes to show what riches there are all over England.

(Source – adapted from www.englishtourism.org.uk)

Q1 *Visit the website of* www.englishtourism.org.uk *and see if you can find out why these awards were given.*

Q2 *Why do you think the winners were selected as being effective enough to receive the awards? What made them more worthy than others to receive the award? What did they do that others didn't?*

Q3 *What benefits will the different organisations receive from winning these awards?*

Q4 *What benefits will the employees of these different organisations receive from the fact that they have won these awards?*

Q5 *Look on the Internet and see if you can find the website of ONE of the winners. Now design a leaflet that they could use to give to potential customers about their organisation.*

case study

The best of English tourism announced

The English tourism Council has now merged with the British Tourist Authorithy to form VisitBritain. For more information visit their website: www.visitbritain.com.

Portfolio-building advice

This unit is internally assessed and you will have to produce a portfolio of work. You will need to study the customer service provided by a leisure or tourism organisation. This could be one that you go to for your work experience, or your teacher might give you a case study about a particular organisation and you can study this.

You will need to produce a portfolio based on your investigations into the situations that require staff to have contact with customers and the way in which the organisation meets the needs of different types of customer. You will also need to collect examples of different types of customer records used by the organisation and show how the organisation deals with complaints. You will have to include the following in your portfolio:

- a description of situations or jobs in the organisation where staff have contact with customers;
- examples of customer records held by the organisation;
- how the organisation meets the needs of different types of customers;
- the methods of communication used by the staff;
- examples of how the organisation would deal with complaints;
- an evaluation of the appropriateness of the customer service provided by the organisation;
- a record of your involvement in real or simulated customer service situations, showing:
  - how you have dealt with a variety of different types of customers;
  - how you have handled customer complaints.

Glossary

Abusive: customers who threaten employees or who swear and show the possibility that they could become violent

ACORN: 'A Classification of Residential Neighbourhoods', a segmentation method that uses the census to create 17 different groups and 55 different types of people

Actual product: the way in which the core product is presented to the customer (a package holiday, a theme park or a movie at a cinema)

After-sales service: looking after customers and dealing with their queries even after the sale has been made (this helps to convince customers that the business cares about them and makes it more likely that they would buy again from the business)

Amateur: this means the opposite of professional and those involved do not get paid

Attitude: your view, feelings or opinion about something

Augmented product: everything that is not to do with the product or the service but makes it easier for the customer to buy and to take the decision to buy, such as paying in instalments for a holiday, knowing that a product has a guarantee or even that the business where they made their purchase has a good reputation for dealing with problems

Brand preference: which brand the majority of customers like to use

Brand switching: when customers decides that they want to try another product (an example could be a person who usually likes McDonald's deciding to eat at Burger King or Pizza Hut instead)

Budget: the amount of money available to a leisure and tourism organisation to spend on marketing

Buying habits: how particular customers purchase things; whether they buy them in a shop, on the Internet or by mail order and how often they buy (does the customer use the leisure facility each week or how many holidays does the customer take each year?)

Catering: providing food and drink for sale to the general public

Census: a 10-yearly government questionnaire that requires every household in the United Kingdom to complete a form and answer basic questions about the number of people living there and type of house and so forth

Coaching: showing the participants of a sport or activity what to do; coaching is also a training method to show employees how to make sure customers receive a good level of service from the organisation

Competition: other businesses or organisations offering similar products or services

Competitive: many different businesses trying to attract the same group of customers

Complaints: a customer who feels that the organisation has not acted correctly might complain in writing, by telephone or personally at the organisation itself

Complimentary: given free

Concessionary: a reduced rate; these rates are often offered to students, young children and those over the age of 60 (women) and 65 (men) years

Confidential: something secret or private to the organisation that should not be seen by others

Conservation area: this refers to a particular part of a town, city or piece of countryside that the country considers too beautiful or too important to change

Core product: the basic product or service, for example a holiday, a day out or entertainment

Corporate event: an event in which a business organisation uses leisure and tourism facilities

Corporate image: the way in which an organisation hopes to be seen and recognised by its customers and the general public

Credit: allowing the customer to spread the cost of paying for products and services over a period of time (this may convince a customer who is not sure about buying to think again)

Credit card: issued to a customer by a bank or building society, it allows the customer to spend money and pay a percentage of the money they owe on a monthly basis. This helps the customer to spread the costs of expensive purchases

Credit terms: offering the customer the opportunity to pay for a product or service over a longer period of time instead of paying the full amount at once

Database: this is a way of keeping a lot of different pieces of information on a computer

Delivery: when customers can expect to receive what they have ordered

Demographics: the study of population changes

Discontinue: stop offering a product or service to customers

Discount: a reduced rate, meaning that a member would pay less than a non-member

Discrimination: treating someone unfairly

Distribution channels: move goods from producers to consumers – they overcome the major time and place gaps that separate goods and services from those who would use them

Duty free: items such as alcohol, cigarettes and perfume that can be purchased on international flights at a lower price, as they do not include tax

Effectiveness: achieving something that one sets out to do

Efficiency: working with the least waste of effort; being competent

Ethnic: relating to different races of people from different places

Ethnic minorities: those of a different culture who make up part of the population of an area, region or country

Exclusive: not shared with anyone else

Expenditure: the money going out of a business

Hiring: paying by the hour or day for the use of equipment that belongs to a centre

Incentive programmes: paying salespeople a bonus or a percentage of every sale that they make

Income: the amount of money earned by an individual or a household

Infomercial: an advertisement that has plenty of information for the customer but is designed to make the customer want to buy after being given all the details

Installation: in the case of products such as satellite dishes or cable TV this is normally done by a professional who does the work for the customer

Intangible service: something that customers buy but cannot take away with them, such as a day in a theme park, an aerobics class or flight

Intermediaries: other businesses that sell products and services on behalf of another business (such as a travel agent selling holidays for a tour operator)

Job description: this explains what the job involves and is useful for matching the right person to that job

Leisure: the time that people have left after they have done all the things that they have to do, for instance when they have finished work or school

Lifestyle: what an individual or household likes doing, such as going out for meals or visiting the cinema; it also includes the hobbies and sports that they enjoy

Listed building: this refers to a house or other building that, because of its great historical importance, cannot be changed by the owner

Marketing: getting the right product to the right people in the right place at the right price using the right promotion

Marketing mix: also known as the 'four Ps': product, place, price and promotion, all the ingredients needed to get the marketing right

Market segmentation: splitting up all customers into groups which have similar characteristics (such as age or gender)

Market share: the amount of a business's products and services sold as a percentage of the total number of products and services sold by all competing businesses

Maximising profit: trying to make as much money as possible by cutting down on costs

Motivated: enjoying work and wishing to do a good job

Needs: essential products and services required by customers (food, housing and transport)

OTH: opportunities to hear – the number of times that an average listener could hear the promotion on the radio station

Participate: take an active part in

Privately run: not owned by a local council but owned by an individual or group of individuals

Product: a product is a physical thing; it is something you pay for and can take away with you, for example a can of drink or a tennis racquet

Product awareness: the process of telling potential customers that the product or service exists

Profits: what is left from a business's income after costs have been paid

Pull strategy: means that the business spends most of its money on advertising and promotion to build up customer demand; if the strategy is successful, consumers will ask retailers for the product, retailers will ask wholesalers, and wholesalers will buy from the business – this is called 'pulling' the product through the distribution channel

Push strategy: the business promotes the product or service to other businesses that sell the products or services direct to the customer; because the business offers a good deal to retailers, the retailer will make more effort to sell their products – this is known as 'pushing' through the distribution channel

Recreation: activities that people enjoy doing during their leisure time

Reliability: able to be trusted and dependable

Representative: a person who works for the organisation and meets the customers to carry out the duties of the organisation

Scale of operations: the number of outlets and the size of the business, such as the number of travel agency shops in a chain across the country

Screen-saver: a moving image on the computer screen that appears if the computer is not used for a few minutes

Segment: a group of customers that have similar characteristics and buying habits

Service: this is a general term used to describe everything other than products that may be sold by an organisation (for example, the hire of a tennis court)

Skills: abilities of employees which help them carry out their work

Suggestion boxes: boxes in the reception area of a tourism and leisure facility where customers can put written suggestions about how the facility could be improved

Supplier: an organisation that provides the business with the items or service it needs, for example, printer paper

Tangible product: something physical that customers can take away with them such as a baseball cap, a stick of rock or a programme

Travel insurance: this is paid by the customer to an insurance company. The travel insurance protects the customer in case of a problem with their holiday, or as a result of their holiday. Such a problem might be loss of suitcases, cancelled flight or illness while away

Visa: some countries require visitors to have a visa as well as a passport; a visa is a document that gives the visitor permission to enter the country for a limited length of time

Wants: products or services desired by customers (entertainment and luxuries, which include holidays)

Warranties (guarantees): the business guarantees that the product or service will do what the business claims it will do, otherwise customers may be able to get their money back

Work shadowing: new employees spending their first few days or weeks with a more experienced employee to learn the job

Index